The 100 CRORE Plan

Don't sell your LIFE for LIVING

PANKAJ JAIN

ISBN 979-8-88667-587-0

CONTENTS

PART – II

PREFACE

Learning something new is not interesting in the beginning. Interest grows gradually like *aap muze achche lagne lage.* Don't read page by page in sequence. Many chapters are independent of each other. Pick any one of the twelve powerful trading strategies and go through it. Apply it practically. The trade may be actual or one may write it on a piece of paper as if you have bought it and write stoploss as well. Check your results after an hour, honestly. Identify your mistakes and rectify them, one by one. All readers are welcome to our YouTube channel with more than 1500 free video lessons with practical demos and 1,80,000 subscribers. This channel will give you detailed information on monthly stock market/commodity MCX for the last 11 years. Don't try to finish this book in two days. Keep reading it every week after first scanning through it, conducting trading experiments simultaneously. This single book can change your life for the better. I have gone straight to the matter without lengthy elaboration deliberately. Why? All of us are busy, with lack of time and a low attention span to focus on reading, ignoring the hundreds of videos available. We are trying to solve the biggest problem of this generation – excess knowledge. It is freely available everywhere, pulling us in all directions. We can do anything we want to, that's why we do nothing at all. I received a book on the share market in 1996 from my friend. I tried hard to read it, but was deterred by the lengthy theoretical definitions of balance sheet and other financial terms. Although I was a good reader, I still couldn't finish reading the book. I concluded that it was not my cup of tea. I couldn't touch the subject for the next seven years. I returned to the stock market for an interesting reason which I will mention later. I felt there were so many missing links for a novice in this field. I always advocate a practical, hands-on approach rather than a theoretical one which is useful only in drawing room conversations.

That's why, I designed my classroom, video courses and books on a completely practical approach. There is nothing useless in a 700-page book, but dinner should not be served at breakfast. Anyone can digest a little in the beginning. One can continue learning something, if it is interesting and applicable in real life from the very first day. Nothing is like rocket science. Start doing anything you want to do, make mistakes, rectify them day by day and keep going. Organic learning is so interesting that no one wants to discontinue. Learning is the real joy of life after all. Such learning started after my first resignation, when I left the guided path and chose my own.

"Waiting to be PERFECT before starting? Just start right now, and you will be PERFECT eventually."

PART – I

WHY MY ENTRY IN THE STOCK MARKET WAS A FORTUNATE ACCIDENT. WHY DO MORE INFORMED FELLOWS PLAY DUMB?

I got my first job as a mechanical engineer at Essar Steel in Hazira, which goes by Arselar Mittal today. My friends have been working there for the last 27 years. I had resigned to follow my passions, writing and travelling. Things were different in 1995 when compared to 2015. It wasn't easy to publish my writing then. My 6000-kilometer bike tour with my friend Hemant Gupta required 10 times more effort. Following your passion wasn't in fashion like it is today. The only question was, "How will you earn? How much will you earn?" I started taking some tuition. I thought about going back to my previous job on half the salary during difficult times.

In such a scenario, I considered the stock market for the first time. My dad held some shares. We had come upon those certificates accidentally during Diwali cleaning. It was Shree Cement. Dad had bought some shares through public issue (IPO) at ₹10 per share in 1990. What to do now? We started looking at possibilities. Shree Cement stock value was ₹180 per share. We were a little excited by this 18 times return. I was so dumb in the field of finance, that when I saw boards like *Indira Security* or *Arihant Security*, I thought these firms provided security guards. This ignorance is simply unimaginable in today's age of the internet, when one knows so many things which are not relevant or useful.

I got a stock broker, thanks to a reference. He told me to dematerialize these shares after opening a demat and trading account. We sent the paper certificate for the dematerialization procedure.

We tracked the stock price daily and felt emotional ups and downs as the price fluctuated. It went up to ₹300, then fell to ₹220. Shit! What a loss? We should have sold it at ₹300. In a few months, we needed funds to buy an old flat. Shree Cement was trading at 350 again by that time. The broker insisted that we hold on to the shares, but middle-class families are keen on controlling life in the short run. We sold the shares instead of breaking a small fixed deposit. So we lost control in the long run. Shree cement trades at ₹32,000 today. We got 35 times return which seemed more than enough, but ₹3200 didn't even seem possible. "Where an ordinary person's imagination ends, the reality of the stock market starts from there only."

STORY OF MY FIRST YEAR OF TRADING

Anyone can enter the stock market/commodity trading business. People are not prepared like mature traders and get trapped in attractive midcap and small cap stocks at the wrong levels. Life doesn't stop if someone loses ₹10,000 out of ₹ 20,000, but many traders have left the market due to shocking results in the beginning itself.

THE FIRST CHEQUE VANISHED PHASE

When I came into the market, it was very difficult for me to buy even a magazine worth ₹ 30. Why should I spend if someone could tell me to do whatever needs to be done? This is the common attitude of a beginner middle-class trader. I reached the screen daily at 9:55 a.m. at the sub broking terminal. Trading on my own computer with my own hands was something I couldn't afford. I bought 20 to 50 stocks with much fear. No one from the outside can imagine this experience. How fast and easily trades are completed on screen. I gained money for two days and lost double the amount on the third day. I bought shares at ₹160 and when it went up to ₹169, I bought more at ₹169 excitedly. Then, it came down to ₹162. I sold it at a loss, repenting. I was doing very small trades but still the loss was ₹3000 in 20 days out of the ₹4000 cheque I had written for the first time. I was frustrated to think that even a small worker brings in ₹100 daily while I was losing ₹200 to ₹300 daily. Was this really a business or gambling as others seemed to say? I will leave this stupid trading business once I recover my losses, I thought. My broker told me I would not be permitted to trade the next day if I didn't write another cheque. I had to accept my mistakes in that do or die situation. **All of us change when there is no way to continue ahead.**

FIRST PROFIT RIDE

The next day, I reached the terminal, bought some stock at ₹190. When it started going up further I bought some more stocks at ₹191. I booked a profit selling 60% at ₹196 and the rest at ₹204. These two trades in the morning and one trade in the evening earned me Rs 4500 for the day. The loss was recovered but who leaves the game after victory? Then, I made profits daily and the volume kept going up. I started buying and selling 2000 shares at a single shot. I thought to close at a profit of ₹8000 to 9000 after speedy, heavy-volume trading and checked trading window. I made a profit of ₹22,000, double the amount I had expected. I had earned more than ₹70,000 in just a week. Every career seemed dull in comparison to my growth rate. I considered myself out of danger now. If I lost ₹5000 to ₹6000 someday, it wouldn't affect me. I forgot to eat and sleep when I incurred losses but it was worse when I made profits. I started reaching the terminal before the market opened. I kept trading in the same heavy volume and the market suddenly reversed. I struggled the whole day after I got trapped but nothing worked that day. I was afraid to lose ₹10,000 but when I checked the net position (alt+f6), the losses were actually ₹27,000. I was totally shocked and couldn't accept it. I reacted at the moment and bought 1000 more shares which fell by ₹9 in just 10 minutes. The total loss was ₹36,000, triple that of what I had expected. I returned home in despair. I was in a hurry to recover all the losses the next day. I placed trades within 10 minutes of the market opening and lost ₹18,000 again. When money goes out the door after gains, it is unbearable. All the passion was depleted. A lost trader was trading like a worthless ritual, and I lost ₹10,000 in the next 20 days. When I came to my senses, I realized that ₹70,000 was more than enough for me in those days. If you lost ₹35,000, I still had ₹35,000 left. I should have waited for the right time and then traded with the money I had left. It would have been better. But the market didn't let me recover even half my losses? I was angry and left the market. The study of the fundamental technical aspects of the stock market seemed fake. One can't read and think useful things in such a state of mind. He must take the right decision at the wrong time. Some old traders say that delivery is better. When I was making profits, I was unwilling to listen to anyone. But you must listen to everyone in bad times. How could I believe their stories if I didn't have similar experiences? It was painful to be a part of the story.

BACK TO A JOB AND FEARFUL INVESTOR PHASE

I returned to my prior business like a wife who goes to her mother's place after a fight with her husband. I started taking some IPO and picked some deliveries of stocks. There was some recovery after a fall in the index. I got some money. Again, I went near the market. Delivery turned into trading unknowingly. There was a mix-up of trading and delivery. If some scrip went down during the day, I had to bring it home. That was my delivery. I started with ₹30,000, part of which was my savings, and I borrowed the rest from my father. He gave me ₹30,000 more after some time. When I earned some profits, I managed to arrange for ₹ 40,000 from somewhere and handed in the cheque. My portfolio value was around ₹1 lac. My sentiments fluctuated with little hope of any returns. It showed +10 to 15,000 gain for a period of two to three months. I justified my work with ₹7000 monthly gains when compared to other jobs. My portfolio comprised midcap companies and the Sensex was going up. Suddenly, midcap and small cap investments started going down. My portfolio value reduced to ₹95,000 and then to ₹90,000. My monthly calculations became senseless now. The SENSEX hit a new high. So, I thought my portfolio would recover again. But its value kept decreasing and hit ₹85,000. I asked my broker whether I should hold or sell my stocks and book losses. He suggested I wait a little more. He didn't ask for more details, so I didn't tell him. The SENSEX started going down finally. The portfolio value was ₹75,000 on the first day, it dipped to ₹65,000 on the second day and ₹45,000 on the third. It was shocking. Everyone suggested that I take delivery of shares and avoid intraday trades. See what delivery had done to me? Trading was better than this. At least I experienced some thrill. I couldn't identify my mistakes this time. I didn't do anything wrong but had to pay a penalty of ₹55,000. I started trading again for recovery. I earned 500 plus the first day and 2000 plus the second day. I calculated that if my profits continued at the same level for the next 40 days, I would recover between ₹60k to ₹70k. I decided my target then.

THE TOTAL HOPELESS PHASE

If I earned ₹400+ some days, I thought it was inadequate for recovery. I needed to earn ₹2,000 plus daily. I did not accept the ₹400 plus; it turned into loss of ₹1000 by the evening. The following day I earned ₹2000+. I lost ₹3000 the next day trying to blindly recover my losses. Whenever I did anything in confusion, I suffered losses most of the time. My debit reached ₹10,000. When the sub broker asked for the cheque, I had to sell deliveries worth ₹10,000. The market was sinking slowly, day by day. It was very painful to be stuck in an unavoidable crisis. Then, the market started showing some recovery. It came back to its old level, but my portfolio value dipped from ₹55,000 to ₹35,000. I felt totally trapped. I realized that if you don't understand the market well, no advice from anyone could help me. I agreed to hold delivery at pick. When the market showed some correction, I kept selling in bottom. I started trading again in the volatile market. This was my second mistake. No one can stick to a good plan without knowledge. When beginners enter the market, they wonder what there is to learn. It just involves buying and selling stocks by pressing a few keys. After four months, they realize that no one can understand such ups and downs. There is no science in it, it's just gambling. After 14 months, when they have witnessed all the market moods – the wild bullish phase, nosediving bear phase, and swinging volatility on the dull screen which puts you to sleep, they start seeing something definite in this indefinite market. That's why I suggest that you closely observe a complete market cycle. If you have been in the market for the last 18 months and bull phase is on with small corrections, then you don't know the market. You know it's single mood only. It's like the courtship period which remains sweet due to the little you know. But one has to be in tune with reality before marriage. After losing ₹40,000 in my portfolio within three days, I came to understand that magazines, websites, training courses and my computer were not expensive. Everyone goes to their mother's place like an angry wife, then she cools down and starts to miss her husband, Mr Market, again. It is the same here. Even if you fight, you can't live far from it, if you've joined hands with Mr. Market.

IS ₹100 CR POSSIBLE BY TRADING ONLINE FOR AN HOUR? UNLIMITED MONEY WITHOUT SELLING YOUR LIFE AND HAPPINESS

One needs huge motivation to initiate something that he has not done till today.

There is a thin line between knowing something and still having confusion about the same thing. Studying something is like heating water. It will become vapour and start rising after 100 degrees. If you don't feel like doing, then you need to study more. You need to take a leap of faith one day to start working. So, we shall start with the magic of a compounding calculator. How can we reach ₹100 crore? Keep the end target in sight and start walking. Do you need to earn ₹5 lac per month?

Not at all. Do one thing. Let's calculate: Initial capital is zero. Put ₹3000 in a monthly savings box for 30 years. The rate of return is 35%.

What is the result?

112 CRORES

Putting aside ₹100 per day is possible even if you have ₹5k to ₹10k as capital, which is less than your smart phone's price. An unemployed youngster spends ₹100 daily on petrol. This works out to ₹35,000 in a single year. No one will stick to the same ₹3000 per month as savings. If you've identified your direction, your motivation, knowledge and earnings will grow exponentially. That's why ₹100 crore is a small figure. It can easily become ₹1000 crore if you honestly work towards growth. Share means taking part, so when you buy the shares or stocks of a company, you become its partner. One needs to know about the business before choosing to buy its shares.

How do you get to know about it?

All data and historical charts are there to show you everything.

What is the problem then?

Why is it that only 6% of the Indian population participates in the stock market, while the US has a 50-60% participation?

Social fear is the main barrier.

If your father and uncle are fearful of the stock market, then it will take years to prepare yourself to give it a first try. There were valid reasons for this fear before the 1992 Harshad Mehta scam. But a story has a very long life. That sad story is still alive in many minds even after 30 years. That's why social change is a very slow process. Thank God, social change can now happen at a quicker pace due to the bombardment of information and technological advancement.

Is share market trading a form of gambling?

If you do anything without understanding it properly it is similar to gambling, whether it is some business, industry or even marriage.

Gambling involves uncertainty. A hard-working farmer faces maximum uncertainty. It should rain. If the rains are sufficient, then pests eat their crops. If the harvest is good, then the market rate may fall dramatically. An IIT or IT student might face such uncertainty. There may have been good demand when they chose to study that branch, but everything may have changed when they graduate four years later. Uncertainty is the only certain thing in life, so one need not fear it. Take calculated risks. There are systematic and unsystematic risks in the stock market.

SYSTEMATIC RISK

This is about the overall market. The overall market is connected to a nation's economy. Some macroeconomic factors affecting the economy are Gross Domestic Product (**GDP) growth rate.** The GDP is the SUM of industrial production + AGRI production growth rate. **IIP numbers** indicate the Integrated Industrial Production numbers. Industries depend on **Political stability** while Agriculture depends on **Rainfall**. **RBI monetary policy** – change in the interest rate decides inflow and outflow of money or liquidity in the stock market.

UNSYSTEMATIC RISK

This pertains to particular stocks. It is measured by the BETA value of the stock. How much and how fast it goes up and down with NIFTY or SENSEX. It is related to the fundamental and technical strength of the particular company. It mainly depends on the **Quarterly results** of a company.

How to handle FEAR while trading or investing?

Not knowing something causes FEAR. I have explained every complex concept related to familiarity. If you don't understand many technical indicators and the typical balance sheet, then don't worry at all. It's quite okay. Focus mainly on the price action for trading. Switch off your TV channel while trading. Don't pay attention to any FREE trading tips or advisories. A trader needs to remember one FACT only…that the future is uncertain. So don't try to predict, instead focus on strategy which will keep you safe in a fluctuating, falling market. Review the 12 BIRDS EYE

VIEW trading strategies at the END of this book. Pick any of them and see the magic. Don't chase each and every news item because it comes with at least a five-minutes lag. That's why half-informed traders are trapped daily in news-based trades. Study brings familiarity. However, study creates more confusion in the beginning. It is difficult to digest and retain so much information. Forget everything. Believe me. Try to forget everything you've gone through, because whatever is useful actually can't be forgotten. One can retain only five to 10% of the total information. There's one thing called EXPERIENCE. Unnecessary baggage is not experience. Such useless baggage kills INTUITION and SPONTANITY.

4 THUMB RULES for 100% success in trading.

1. Trade less frequently, earn solid profits.

2. Test the small volume model. Keep fine-tuning it and scale up.

3. Fifty percent of your capital invested must earn a 200% profit. Less capital earns more profits due to more control and less fear.

4. Count timewise returns in percentage. An average 4 percent weekly return is 200% annually.

FOUR TYPES OF MARKET STUDIES

1. Premarket study: This study is done between 8:00 am and 9:00 am, just before the current trading session opens.

2. Running market study: A fast and ultra-focussed study when the market is running (between 9:15 am and 3:30 pm.)

3. Post-market study: Analyse all the mistakes of the day and prepare market watch for tomorrow.

4. Parallel study for long-term portfolio: Get a helicopter view of the domestic and global markets over the last few decades.

There are many sources for your study:

1. **Websites**

    Vast and unlimited knowledge is available. Some websites are updated every minute and some at the end of the day. The list is given below. The trader must browse the internet for Sensex, 20-year charts of stocks, MF, options, technical, fundamentals and global markcts.

2. **Youtube and Instagram/Facebook**

    So many videos are available free of cost. If you want to avoid confusion then go for focussed paid courses.

3. **Newspapers**

    Financial newspapers give day-to-day details. The Economic Times, Financial Express, and Business Standard are the main newspapers.

4. **TV news channels**

    CNBC, ZEE Business, NDTV Profit are the main channels to watch. TV channels are louder than all other sources and can be used with our routine. Be careful of 24*7 noise and hidden motives of the media.

5. **Books and Magazines**

Dalal streets and Capital Market are the best magazines, both offline and online. Their detailed scoreboards and quarterly reports are good. Google search stock market books and go through the summary on the summary.com website.

6. **Paid courses**

We have one hour to one year courses. If a trader takes a small course every day or every week, it will still be worth it. If someone spends ₹1000 daily or ₹3 lacs a year, then profit will reach a minimum of ₹9 lacs. It's not about learning something once, but practicing daily. This will help you build the right trading habits.

TOP stock market websites to know everything about day trading and investments

- www.moneycontrol.com

  It is a very good website to study equity, futures, options, commodities, currency, crypto currency, personal finance and mutual funds. The app is also very good.

- In.investing.com

  This is an international website with the best speed. The technical analysis is also very good.

- www.economictimes.com

  It is available in Hindi and English. ET is the most reputed brand name when it comes to financial newspapers.

- www.earnometer.com

  This is a simple and good website to scan technical analysis of any scrip pertaining to stocks, commodities or the currency market.

- www.nseindia.com

This is the official website of the National Stock Exchange. It's the first website any Indian market trader must go through.

- www.bseindia.com

This is the official website of the Bombay Stock Exchange. It's the basic website that any Indian market trader must become familiar with.

- www.motilaloswal.com

This site offers an option chart for any strike price and has a user-friendly results calendar.

- www.topstockresearch.com

You can check all the technical indicators of any stock showing some positive or negative technical breakout in a single page to compare and decide really fast.

- www.profit.ndtv.com

This is the most useful website to trade intraday with more systematic stock screeners like recovery form low or near 52-week high.

- www.trendlyne.com

Study the fundamental and technical screeners at one place to help you pick the right stock both ways. Study the portfolios of India's superstar investors here.

THE ABCS OF THE STOCK MARKET

- **Advances /Declines** – Number of shares showing gains / losses today.

- **AMC** – Asset Management Company. MF has various schemes.

- **A group stocks** – Grouping of stock as per quality such as A, B, T, TS and Z.

- **BSE** – Bombay Stock Exchange since 1875.

- **Gainer/loser** – Gain in price/loss in price today with respect to the previous close.

- **Index** – Average price of the selected group of shares showing market mood.

- **ISIN** – International Security Identification Number. It's unique.

- **Bonus** – Non cash corporate benefit in the form of additional shares.

- **Dividend** – Corporate cash benefit shared as percentage of face value.

- **Split** – Both market price and face value split for more participation.

- **ROCE** – Return on capital employed.

- **Percent Variance** – Net profit or sales change from the previous quarter or financial year.

- **Sensex** – Sensitive Index comprising top 30 stocks from major sectors.

- **NIFTY** – Top 50 stocks' price average from all major sectors.

- **Nifty 200** – Top 200 shares from large cap and midcap stocks as well.

- **Midcap** – Medium level companies with bigger risks and bigger returns.
- **Small caps** – Small companies with biggest risks and returns.
- **Most active** – Scrips traded with maximum volume.
- **BE (trade to trade)** – allowed to trade in delivery only.
- **Bulk deal** – A large number of shares traded in a single trade.
- **Contract note** – Document with every detail of a particular day's trade.
- **NSCCL** – National Stock Clearing Corporation Limited.
- **NSE** – National Stock Exchange from 1992, after SEBI Regulation Act, 1992.
- **NCFM** – NSE Certification in Financial Market.
- **SEBI** – Securities and Exchange Board of India.
- **ETF** – Exchange Traded Funds (traded in secondary markets like stocks).
- **LTP** – Last traded price.
- **NAV** – Net Asset Value (Price of 1 MF unit computed daily after close).
- **Square off** – Bringing net position to zero by selling bought shares or buying short shares.
- **Redemption** – Selling MF units in parts or all units.
- **Depository** (NSDL/CDSL) – Investor's demat holding from NSE/ BSE are safe with these government agencies.
- **Only buyers** (Upper circuit) – maximum price allowed on a trading day.
- **Only sellers** (Lower circuit filter) – minimum price allowed in a day.
- **Volume** – Number of shares traded.
- **Volume shockers** – Sudden spike in volume due to some good/bad news.

- **Open interest** – one outstanding buy + sell trade in F&O is termed one OI.

- **Turnover** – Amount traded

- **DIP** – Sudden sell and recovery or vice-versa is called DIP.

- **Trailing stoploss** – Upgrade SL when price goes further in one trend.

- **Crash** – All round heavy selling which occurs once in two to three years.

- **Pullback rally** – market goes upside with big rally after a big downfall.

- **SIP** – Systematic investment plan to buy MF or equity weekly or monthly.

- **TTM** – Trailing 12 months.

- **Scrip code** – NSE/BSE

- **Quarterly numbers** (Timahi results)

- Mar-Apr/Jun-Jul/Sep-Oct/Dec-Jan are when companies disclose quarterly SALES and PROFIT figures.

- **VIX** – Volatility index. When Nifty makes bottom, VIX will make picks. Thus, when VIX breaks resistance in charts, the trader should sell NIFTY futures or BUY PUT.

- **Bracket order** – It comprises in-built STOPLOSS and TARGET.

- **Cover order** – In-built stoploss defined by us.

- **Trigger price** – Stoploss orders must have two prices. Trigger selling price in SELLING stoploss. Trigger buying price in BUYING SL. TRIGGER is always between current market price and stoploss price.

- **T+2** – Settlement of shares after two days of trade.

- **M2M** – Mark to Market. It shows gains or losses.

- **MIS** – Margin intraday square off.

- **CNC** – Cash and carry to take delivery of stocks

- **NRML** – Normal order used to take overnight position in FnO/mcx fut.

STOCK MARKET VERSUS ANY TRADITIONAL BUSINESS

All traditional businesses have entry barriers. They need ₹5 to ₹50 lacs capital. The maximum profit one can expect is between 25 to 40% of capital after cutthroat competition and long working hours.

The stock market is the mother of all businesses. So it will not be outdated regardless of whether businesses change all the time. One can start with ₹5000 only. This means anyone can afford this from anywhere around the globe. A one to two percent daily profit is possible on average. This means no one will gain five days a week or 250 trading days a year.

There will certainly be days of losses despite all the knowledge and discipline. But the stock market / commodity mcx trade can give you a 100 to 300% gain annually with just an hour of online trading daily.

Stock market versus any other professional course or job

If you want to become a doctor, engineer, lawyer or chartered accountant, then you need to study for 15 to 20 years, at least. Few may get jobs easily; many may not get good jobs with proper salaries. All these professional courses cost a minimum of ₹5 to ₹15 lacs for trainee's fees and monthly maintenance. So a professional depends on many agencies like companies, colleagues and clients for growth and opportunities.

The stock market can be learned online completely. Starting with free videos, move on to a small paid course for as low as ₹999. One doesn't need any certificate or degree to become a successful trader or investor. No one is dependent on the share market. You can choose your work hours, risk level and lifestyle. Trading and investments can be done parallel with any other career. So, if your salary is used as a scholarship for a business, then you are not only growing but there's also hope for unlimited expansion in life.

You need not change your profession or business to learn the stock market. It can be done simultaneously with any job or study. It's good if you are busy. It is okay to be lazy too, because one trade daily done in five minutes can be a winning formula.

Your basic profession helps to maintain a safe distance from the market screen other than the best trading hours. TIMING and TARGET discipline are pillars of a successful trading career.

THERE ARE 6 WAYS TO PARTICIPATE IN THE STOCK MARKET

How should a beginner start?

1. Primary market – IPO/FPO

    Secondary Market –

2. Day trading (trading on the same day needs more study and skill)

3. Short term or swing trading (holding shares from 1 day to 1 year)

4. Longterm investment (holding shares for more than 1 year)

5. Futures and options (trading in LOTS – very big scale – most risky)

6. Indiret investment – MUTUAL FUNDS

MUTUAL FUNDS

Mutual funds are the institutions that avail systematic benefit of equities with the expertise of their Fund Managers. Ninety-five percent of retail traders are unable to maintain profitable disciplines with their tiny funds, but MF managers handle funds of ₹1000 crores to ₹1 lac crores. So the study of mutual funds gives us a solid basis to trust the stock market for the next 10 to 40 years or even longer. We can study the TOP holdings of any mutual fund scheme, it's comparative chart with benchmark index and the buying and selling patterns with proper diversification. They BUY in dips and SELL on picks like Smart Money. Retail traders' investment is known as FOOL's money, because they BUY on picks without diversification and sell in DIPS, feeling trapped repeatedly.

Is it better to invest in mutual funds or direct equity / stocks

Start with 70 percent in mutual funds and 30 percent in equity. The Sensex goes down for technical correction every three to six months. One should focus on studying and comparing the right stocks in the right sector from mutual fund portfolios. Mutual funds fall moderately in comparison to equity so I suggest that you fall with mutual funds and rise with equity. This means, if the Net Asset Value of 10 goes down to 9 when the market falls, the equity will drop from 10 to 6 in the same fall. So sell your mutual funds at this moment and invest in equity bit by bit. The switching will be mild if you don't do it in a single shot. This is because no one can identify the exact bottom. It may continue to fall even after your entry. One can buy put or sell call to hedge big equity portfolios in the falling market. Keep booking part profits on each market jump. Initially, the MF/EQ ratio will be 60/40, then 50/50 and finally 40/60. When the mutual fund increases from 9 to 10, then equity will go up from 6 to 10 at the same time.

So, fall with MF and rise with equity.

Small and midcap may be bought in bottom, but balance these with large cap stocks as well.

How should a beginner start?

Below is the right sequence for a beginner to start, Swing trading is safest for the beginner with direct involvement, then the risk increases gradually in further trading instruments. Stock futures is the most risky trading instrument.

- **Swing trade**
- **MF sip**
- **Intraday trade**
- **Nifty option**
- **Stock option**
- **Nifty – bank nifty future**

- **Stock future**

Long term direct equity investment should be made simultaneously. Equity portfolio for long-term should not be avoided at all. All other ways are optional but small, regular, long-term investments is life changing. Thus, it is a must for everyone.

There are two sections of the stock market

Primary market – When any company goes public and allots shares to investors directly.

IPO – Initial public offer

FPO – Follow on public offer

IPO strategy for best short-term returns

Watch all the closed IPOs for oversubscription and select three to five oversubscribed IPOs with their mutual funds holding. Chittorgarh. com is a good website for IPOs. Start accumulating in the next three to six months. This can give you very fast, big profits. IPOs have the novelty benefit and their actual price discovery will happen in the Nifty or Sensex crash.

FPO – Stocks which are already listed in the secondary market and are issued again as new shares. FPO has a stock price already there, so these won't give listing gains. Firm allotments might be there means you are applying for 20 bid lots and getting all the lots where as one gets 1 or 2 lots in case of 20 lots IPO application.

The Secondary Market

When shares are issued to investors and the stock is listed in the stock market. Anyone can buy or sell at the current market price from the screen online. Intraday trading, swing or short-term trading or long-term investments come under the secondary market. Derivatives (futures and options) are also directly connected to the secondary market. Equity Mutual funds are indirect investments in the stock market because we are going through some AMC and their fund managers.

FIVE MAIN ASSET CLASSES:

Do you work for money or does your money work for you?

Fixed deposits / post office: These are the most prevalent types of investments even in remote villages. They gave great returns 30 years back. In the 80s, they gave a 14 to 15% return but now it has reduced to a mere 6%. So FDs/RDs are more about safety than returns.

Insurance: There are endowment, moneyback, term, Mediclaim and ULIP (Unit Linked Insurance Plan) policies. ULIPs mean investing in equity, but the investment is locked for a period. One can avail the switching facility to DEBT, but if someone can handle the switching properly, then why shouldn't he/she go for direct equity or mutual funds with total freedom and much bigger returns?

It's not good to mix insurance with investments. So go with TERM insurance for pure insurance purposes which has an annual premium of ₹7k to ₹8k for a ₹50 lac risk cover depending on your age. Invest the remaining 70 to 80% of the premium in midcap or small cap mutual fund schemes for at least 1000% extra returns.

Real Estate-

Real Estate or property investment is a very big and powerful investment but it's not that organised, transparent and needs substantial market study. There are legal issues, it requires skilled negotiations and huge cash flow. However, owning a home is like Social Nirvana in Indian society. Builders earn a heavy premium due to this blind social push. Home loans and tax exemptions are winning features, but one needs to understand the whole game. That's why we have launched the REAL ESTATE & property broking course as well.

Equity and MF:

Equity investments are accepted lately in Indian society. Thanks to the decreasing interest rates and increasing awareness, Indians have started to participate in the share market knowingly or unknowingly with 10 to 20% of total capital going to ULIPs.

Precious metal: Our society is blindly fascinated with gold. Gold and property are tangible, thus they are more trusted. Few Indians are able to protect the gold jewellery they wear. Gold chains are frequently snatched on the road. But they are more afraid of stock market risks. It's ridiculous! Gold and silver have intrinsic value when the value of equity is questioned. But quality is an issue. It needs physical handling, involves locker costs and there are unfair price gaps between screen and spot price. Sovereign gold or gold ETFs are better options but gold has given a 9 to 10% return in the last 40 years which is just half of equity returns.

Cryptocurrency: Tech savvy people with a fast-growth mindset are attracted to this recent asset class. This might be a gamechanger for the future but there is confusion right now. Every asset class will be deemed suspicious by the masses in the beginning, just like when banks, insurance or equity were introduced. Every asset class shows a five-year cycle generally.

So, don't love or hate any of them; there should be a **proper allocation** as per your GOALS. INFLATION is the common enemy, so you will have to beat it. It may be five to six percent on paper but10 to 11% in reality, in the age of instant loans and exponentially growing expenditures. EQUITY or the stock market is the only hope for investors to beat inflation in the long run. The share market has given 18% returns in last 40 years.

RULE OF 110

It tells us how much of one's capital should be allocated to equity to beat inflation. Subtract your age from 110. If your age is 25, then 110 – 25 = 85.

So 85% of your capital should be in equity. If your age is 60, then 110 – 60 = 50.

So 50% of your capital should be in equity, because there are fewer years available to accommodate financial cycles.

HOW TO START TRADING FOR BEGINNERS?

If you want to enter the stock market, the most frequent question is where to start and what is the right sequence of the various tasks involved.

1. Check if you have a pan card. If you don't have one, apply for it. You can search for an agency on google.

2. Search online for stockbrokers in your area. There should be sub brokers with an office set up nearby or some discount brokers online. I suggest you go to some nearby trading set up to just be familiar with day-to-day trading operations and terminology.

3. Be prepared with a cancelled bank cheque leaf attached to your savings account, photos, address proof and identity proof. You will need to pay a nominal account opening fee. It may be from INR 300 to 800, but this doesn't matter at all.

4. Then, invest in a set of books and a video course and start watching during your spare time. Take the 72 hour whole sole market moto. This will be a good place to start.

5. Meanwhile, your trading account will be processed. Download the trading app of your broker on your smartphone and login with the given password and user ID. Get the trading set up on your laptop free of cost through *emmy* or *showmypc* screen sharing software with the help of the broker's IT staff.

6. Transfer a small capital to your trading account. It could be anywhere between Rs 5,000 to Rs 20,000 in the beginning.

7. Start buying and selling orders with nominal volumes because you will make many mistakes in the beginning. You should not waste big money while you are learning the basics of the stock market.

8. Choose the most simple and basic strategy for the first 10 days. Then, start trying other strategies, one by one. You will become comfortable in placing orders, watching the screen and taking immediate actions.

9. Focus on equity cash first (low to high volume) Then nifty option/ bank nifty call put, nifty future and bank nifty future. Try one trade a day in stock option first on paper, then actual. Then, move on to stock futures. Finally, try single stock futures with hedging per day. There is a big dip every quarter. Plan your next big step only after such a big dip.

Good short-term strategy

1. **Near 52-week high stocks:** When you check out the equity stocks on the NSE India website, you will see Nifty, Nifty Next 50, and Nifty midcap list. Recently, broken high is in dark green. Just note down the stocks from these three lists. Then, see if nifty's one-month and three-month charts are supporting. Keep these shares in mind. Then, observe the sectors. According to the sectors, you can make call/put combo for three to four days or BTST in call/put. (Refer to Pankaj Jain's stock market YouTube channel for more details). Just look for a combo situation where the stock price is near a 52-week high but is down in the last 30 days. This is safe and promising. Accumulate these stocks in gradually increasing quantities in the forthcoming big dips. Review MF holdings to select better quality stock. It will give better profits quickly and with minimum risk.

PROFIT calculations for swing trading

Capital required

Lower end: ₹1 lac {30k+30k+30k)

Upper end: ₹6 lacs (2k+2k+2k in each stock)

Monthly profit expected is 5%. This works out to: 30,000 * 12 = ₹3.6 lacs

If monthly profit expected is 10%, it is 60,000 * 12 = ₹7.2 lacs

You can't manage to earn the same profits regularly but with a 5% return in a month, you will get between 20% to 30% returns in the next month only. If one has a delivery turnover of less than ₹1 crore, buy +1 crore sell, then no audit is required by the CA. One can start experimenting even with a capital of ₹10,000 but see the results in percentage. If one earns ₹60,000 on ₹1 lac capital, then he has to pay 10% short term capital gains tax. Ten percent of 60,000 = 6000 only, which is very little in taxes in comparison to other businesses.

Two main screeners for two main swing trading styles

1. Monthly loser nifty 100 stocks for defensive swing trade (expected profits + 5% monthly)

2. All time high nifty 500 for aggressive swing trading (5% weekly)

TAXATION

When you trade intraday, it is considered a business. Business income will be taxed like any other business as per the income slabs. Income taxes will depend on one's gains or losses, but business taxes are always there on every trade.

STT – Security Transaction Tax

- **Turnover charges**

- **Delivery charges**

I suggest you trade for ₹10,000 value or 1 lot future/option to see the tentative cost of brokerage and taxes per ₹1 lac turnover.

Short term trade: In short term trade, one needs to take delivery. If you buy ₹1 crore and sell ₹1 crore trading value, then you need to submit an audit report for more than ₹2 crores delivery in a single year. Short term capital gains tax is 15% on gains. Trading losses of an individual may be adjusted for the next seven years. Long term capital gains tax is 10% on gains, but if it is less than ₹1 lac, it may be exempted.

If one is trading in futures and options, then it is also like business income. But security transaction taxes and turnover charges are heavy. The trader needs to pay a 10-20% margin only for trading but taxes are calculated on total turnover value. So heavy trading in nifty/bank nifty or stock futures and options might erode all your capital without big losses.

Trade repair in intraday / short term

Admit your mistakes and they will go away. If you justify them, they will penetrate deep down into your personality. If you buy 1000 shares and their value is dropping, sell 400, then 200 more shares at the lower price. Cut down the losing position.

If Nifty is still near it's day's low, sell the weakest share and buy other stocks / sectors that are going up. Position yourself with strict stop loss. Keep a stoploss cap in mind. If it touches 1000 or 2000, just stop. Wait for the next time slot, 1:54 to 2:29 p.m.

In case of short term trading, sell half the quantity, switch to other sectors or wait for a dip to re-enter. In this way, you control your losses in holdings and gain profits in the current opportunities. So, the trade gets repaired gradually and you can exit from it with profit or cost to cost in harder times.

INTRADAY TRADE REPAIR

If you follow my strategies, then you are less likely to trap yourself in some big loss, but suppose you don't follow them and find yourself in the middle of some big loss, I have some wonderful trade repair methods. Basic principles of trade repair:

1. Stop or control the loss making position.

2. Wait for any right opportunity from other sectors.

3. You can change your direction (buying to selling)

    Or change trading instruments from high risk to low risk. (Stock futures to stock options, or options to equity cash)

4. Cover losses in three to four shots.

5. Don't repeat the same mistakes that caused your losses and suffer bigger losses.

For example, suppose you buy a share at ₹180, and there was a sudden reversal in the sector or Nifty/Sensex. Consequently, the stock price falls to ₹150. Reduce the quantity from 500 to 200 first. Don't cost average in panic. If it happened in the morning slot (9:15 to11:30 a.m.), then wait till 1:20 p.m. The stock may touch the support, then retest it. Nifty might bottom out in the next 30 to 60 minutes. Buy 700 shares in parts near support. Take SL of 50 paisa only. If it shows 2 to 4% short covering after a 12% downfall, 700 shares will recover ₹2000 from a total loss of ₹4000. The rest should be recovered in forthcoming trade sessions with tightly calculated risks only. Suppose you hold the entire quantity and it dips by 12%. You will suffer a huge loss. Traders generally exit at the worst bottom price, illogically waiting for the price to fall. Don't sell in panic if the price dips from ₹170 to ₹150. Just check on the average traded price. If it is ₹158, then place selling orders at anywhere between

₹155 and ₹157 in parts. It will touch that price to hunt stop loss of short sellers and you will get a better price. This will boost your confidence. So, it may be possible to short sell the stock when it falls from ₹157 to ₹155 to ₹145. If you don't place prior orders, then you won't be able to take decisions and place sell orders quickly at the moment of short covering spike. Sometimes, traders buy more shares at ₹155 to ₹157 to cost average, hoping for a total recovery of the stock price. This silly mistake will double the losses and reduce your confidence and mental balance. So, big money is based on many small things.

A full day of trading with entry and exit (All strategies in the right sequence)

What to keep in mind before entering a TRADE? I have given the timing for all trading instruments like futures, options or equity here. But FOCUS on a single instrument at a time to win. For example, Nifty option for 10 days and measure the results, equity intraday with all-in-one screeners and measure results.

1. Study the global markets weekly or daily (whatever is available on money.rediff.com or in.inveting.com, moneycontrol.com/ Bloomberg)

2. Identify the top monthly and last day losers/gainers stocks.

3. Observe yesterday's gaining and losing sectors.

4. See the Nifty/Sensex last five-day chart.

5. See last five-day chart for loser stocks.

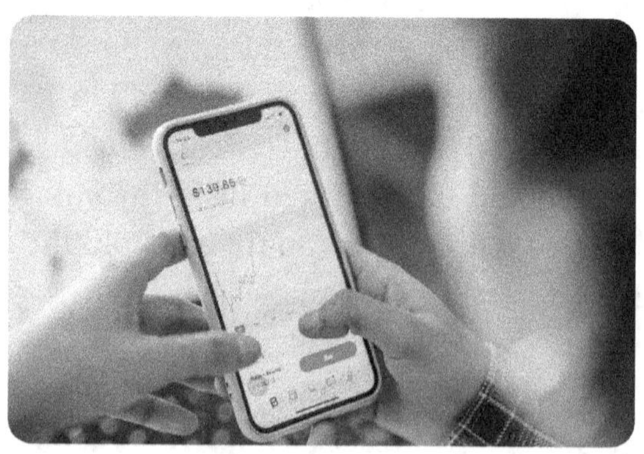

6. See Nifty/bank nifty's most active call/put and note it down on paper. Buy nifty futures or keep SL, buy above high in call+ put, if the last two days showed a clear jump or fall.

7. See monthly loser stocks call and monthly gainer stocks put and their hedging.

8. Place buy/sell on nifty gainer/loser at current market price (cmp) with 1% stoploss or see volume screener/hourly gainer/ recovery from intraday low in way2wealth.com/moneycontrol. com.

    Use these screeners for best intraday stock picks:

    Bulk deal by mutual funds

    Volume increase price rise

    Recovery from intraday low

    Buy top gainers/sell top losers with low volume and book on move till 11:00 a.m.

9. Keep STOPLOSS buy above high in top gainer of midcap and stoploss sell below low in top loser of midcap. Book fast in activated trade. (Equity or call/put)

10. Take a break from 11:30 a.m. to 1:30 p.m. (Enjoy lunch, study, run errands).

11. Check nseindia.com. See top gainer and top loser sectors and stocks or ALL in ONE 3:25 p.m. screener.

12. Place buy above high and sell below low in (equity or option) or see volume screener/hourly gainer/recovery from intraday low in way2wealth.com/moneycontrol.com/. Buy top gainers/sell top losers with low volume.

13. Place order in Nifty/ bank Nifty futures with hedging of call/ put or place trade in nifty call + put combo daily at 1:54 p.m. stoploss 8 points.

14. Try to make all your booking before 3:00 p.m.

15. See volume screener again for BTST trade and buy at 3:29 p.m. and sell at 9:16 a.m. the following day or see nseindia.com for BTST trade in options of Nifty/bank Nifty or strong/weak stocks.

16. Check the order book, trade book and net position every 30 minutes. Remove useless orders. Keep booking part profits on each move.

17. Sell/buy (square off) extra position in post market from 3:40 to 4:00 p.m.

18. Note down your trading record with tentative brokerage fees, taxes and analyse your mistakes today to improve in the following day's trading.

4 STEPS FOR SUCCESSFUL ONLINE TRADING (MCX/ NSE)

When you start trading, you should follow four steps.

LOW VOLUME, LOW MARGIN

Buy shares worth anywhere between ₹1000 and ₹5000 only. No big losses or gains, just study. Start trading with micro, gold Guinea, set a small target of 0.25%. This phase is useful in studying the behaviour of any scrip.

LOW VOLUME, HIGH MARGIN

Buy shares worth anywhere between ₹10k to ₹20k and wait for the BIG move. Trade with micro/mini lots, but set a big target…1% of the income to start with. Practice for months at this level.

HIGH VOLUME, LOW MARGIN

Buy shares worth anywhere between ₹1 lac and ₹3 lacs and book fast at 1 to 2% only. Trade with three to four lots but set a small target: 0.25% to 0.5% only. The suitable time for this is between 10:00 a.m. to 10.30 a.m. and 2p.m. to 2.30p.m. This step will allow you to earn between ₹5k to ₹10k in just an hour.

HIGH VOLUME, HIGH MARGIN

Buy futures or options on any big reversal once a month only. Trade with three to four lots and set a big target of 1 to 2%. For example, positional calls or clear breakouts such as recent breakouts in gold from 24k to 26k in three days. If you want to keep growing in the market, then do not rush. Follow these steps for a few months. Success will be quite predictable.

TRADERS GEETA

Equity + FnO + Commodity mcx trading

Important tips to earn in mcx / stock market trading?

1. Two things are most important.

    The technical aspects to understand the basic direction of chart discipline: **Time Discipline + Target Discipline.** Whenever there are big fluctuations, it attracts all traders back. When traders come back to trade, it becomes rangebound again. Just notice the last Friday's free fall followed by the very dull movement on Saturday, Monday and Tuesday morning. When 90% of the traders become hopeless, it moves up 2000 points in four hours.

2. Beginners are hyperactive. They try to trade on every up and down. Mature traders choose 10 trades in a week. If chance goes away its okay, but capital should not go away. So, calculate the number of trades and stop losses you can afford. Suppose there is a positional buy call in nickel above 1052 SL 1034 (18pt = 4500) tgt1100. A small trader can't afford it but he wants to do so. He should use ₹3-3 SL 3 times.

    Buy at 1052, SL 1049

    Buy at 1043, SL 1040

    Buy at 1037, SL 1034

    In this way, it is possible to trade such calls with an SL of just ₹9.

3. How were the global markets last night? (Check yahoo.finance. com). See trade set up for tomorrow and what changed in market

overnight articles to make a broad outline of trading volume and trading instruments (equity, futures or options).

4. Watch the stock market at 9:00 a.m., just before it opens. Check Nifty/Sensex,

   SGX nifty (Singapore) and Nasdaq, Dow Jones (US) in the global market when it opens at 10:00 a.m. First, see the direction of the Comdex index at the top right of your screen.

5. Check market watch before 9:00 a.m. created after yesterday's market close at 4:00 p.m., from 3:25 p.m. all in one screener. Observe monthly and yearly breakout stocks from NIFTY100 and midcap-small cap shares from short-term breakout chartink.

6. See NIFTY100 or SENSEX top GAINERS/LOSERS from BSE HEATMAP. Place six to 10 scrips on market watch on one screen and keep the nifty chart open on another. Smartphones are suggested for mobility and big smart TV screens or laptops to run charts and screeners.

7. You can start test trade with micro silver at 10.01 a.m. It is possible to have 150 points in silver in the first three minutes. But do it with strict SL. When you become confident for seven days in silver micro then do it with mini 5kg or 30kg. For this it is necessary to have a keyboard and operating skills. Buy silver at ₹51,900, SL ₹51,750, TGT ₹52,100. Place all orders fast. After gaining confidence, three big lots give you ₹15,000 in the first three minutes. Never do it without strict stoploss.

8. Your reaction time is very important in trading. How many minutes do you take to make a decision and execute the trade?

9. Don't be emotional when stoploss hits. It is better to hit 5 SL of 150 points rather than 1 SL of 1000 points.

10. Be flexible in trading. Suppose silver goes up in the morning and down in the afternoon and up again in the evening, then the flexible trader takes 200 points from each 500 points in the safe zone.

11. Never try to chase any commodity till pick or bottom. Place prior orders for profit booking. Book at bottoms and resell again at jumps or if it breaks low (always with SL).

12. Keep time discipline. Trade from 10:00 a.m. to 11:00 a.m. Check opportunities at 2:00 p.m. when the European market settles after opening. Six to 7:00 p.m. is the best time for mcx commodities due to LME opening time.

13. Target discipline. Fix a minimum of 2% daily TGT on capital. Every trader is not supposed to trade on every call. You can have 6000 in 3 safe calls with small SL.

14. The target for maximum losses in a day should also be fixed with a profit TGT. Trading every hour will not give you any profits. Just learn to digest profits or losses. Take rest for two hours or two days after small/big losses. Check this website to see annual commodity charts.

    In.investing.com

    Commodity section

    www.mcxindia.com See all products, details and fundamentals (demand and supply). If you have a problem with English, check the commodity section of this site: www.economictimes.com/hindi.

15. Do not get irritated when you hit stoploss. Always calculate the amount of stoploss instead of the number of stop losses.

16. If there is a clear reason to buy something like monthly or yearly high breakout then buy it with affordable volume with strict stoploss. If buyers suddenly decrease, then don't wait for SL to hit, just exit.

17. Keep booking part profits and keep trailing SL with the remaining volume.

18. For bigger profits, you need to do one thing only: Control your losses. Profits will take care of itself. So place proper stop losses and leave the screen for 40 minutes at least.

19. Traders make one common mistake. They control their profits, but wait in their losses. There should be a 1:3 SL/profit ratio.

20. When you open positions, just calculate the value of total stop losses. If the total stop loss amount is higher, then reduce the volume.

21. Control over volume is the ultimate control. If you make three mistakes in a micro lot, then recovery is possible in a single big lot.

22. Do not over trade. If daily losses reach 2% of capital, then stop trading immediately. It is the MOST IMPORTANT RULE. And it takes time to practice it.

23. Just learn to digest profits or losses. Take a break, listen to music, go to the market, meet people or study old charts on the internet.

24. Always think in percentages. If silver moves 500 points then it is just 1%. It may go up to 6% someday.

25. Beginners are hyperactive, but mature traders trade only when there is strong reason.

26. Learn to trade with time discipline; twice or thrice a day is ideal (say between 9:40 a.m. and 1:40 p.m. for stocks, and at 5:40 p.m. for MCX). If you learn to remain calm in red and blue then you will win definitely.

27. Calculate your daily brokerage rates and taxes. You can't ignore detailed costs in any business. Traders generally pay up to ₹1000 a day in brokerage fees and taxes, but they never calculate this. That is why they are not mentally prepared to pay half of this for good research and training.

28. Just record all your trades in a pocket diary and analyse your trading behaviour and methodology day by day. Facts and figures give us the exact picture. Do not argue and do not justify your mistakes. Accept them simply and rectify them day by day.

29. A trader's core thinking is very important. If you think that you are gambling, then it becomes gambling actually. If you consider

it to be a genuine business, then you are ready for all proper inputs.

30. Let go of your ego and keep your profits. Keep your ego and leave your profits. A trader has to be very flexible. He should adjust profits and losses as per market conditions.

31. Try to trade in the safe zone. If copper goes up from ₹400 to ₹410, then take ₹403 to ₹407. This is a safe zone. You can go for three lots for a 12pt profit.

32. Do not chase profits. If the opportunity goes, let it go. It will come back. But if capital goes, it will not come back. No one dies if he falls from a slow moving bicycle. Speed without skill is a big danger. Your growth should be slow and steady to be successful.

33. You should not be bullish or bearish by nature. If you are occupied with some presumption, you cannot see actual movement.

34. Reduce your reaction time. If you observe continuously without any pressure then it will reduce automatically. Reaction time means the gap between taking a decision and implementing the trade.

35. Do not become a dustbin. The media, TV channels, newspapers, co-traders and many websites make contradictory statements. One becomes full of garbage like a dustbin, totally confused. Refrain from noise, listen to everyone but follow the right reasons.

36. Do not buy or sell on an impulse. If the right reasons are there (sector running, above average, more buyers, bounce from bottom) buy/sell optimum volume with strict small stoploss. If no right reason is there, sit free the whole day without any trade or open hedging on both sides (up/down).

37. You should not be attached or detached to any share or commodity. Some fellows say that we trade in bullions only. Others say, "I will never touch silver again." WHY? We should be familiar with all commodities especially in the MCX to avail regular intraday profits. If gold/silver show very good moves for

two to three days, then it will become rangebound for the next four to five days. When the bullion takes a breather, base metals like copper, nickel, lead and zinc show big moves, one by one. Choose the strongest to buy and the weakest to sell on that day to earn maximum with minimum risk.

38. Many traders know how to trade when the market is good but few know how to pass time without any trades when the market is confusing and in a tight range.

39. Keep checking all your pending orders by clicking F3-f3 and cancel all useless orders. See net position (ALT+F6) and keep booking profits directly from there.

40. We need to try and test the right system for 50 days. Just learn to maintain 1000 in the evening (7:00 p.m. – 8:30 p.m. slot). Then multiply lots (2.3.6) gradually. PROFIT may reach up to ₹5,000 or ₹10,000 daily. If you reach such targets in 24 months, then is it late? ₹2 lac per month within 2 years must be great growth rate.

41. Some days, you may try hard but still end up with a loss of ₹2000, hitting SL. Just accept it and leave the screen for the day. You don't have any burden of loans, salaries, electricity bills or petrol, etc. Play it cool.

42. Never try to recover losses in a single shot. Otherwise, your losses may double. Recover losses of ₹10,000 in four parts.

43. Even if you have lost ₹20 lacs, it is okay to plan to trade for ₹5000 daily but stick to the plan. You will cover all your losses in 400 days (less than 18 months). If you need to get training, become a salaried share dealer. Arrange all the trading tools. Within 20 days, it will be clear to you whether these things are working or not.

44. Record all your trading activities and time slots during the dull hours or late evening. You will be able to identify loopholes and improvise day by day.

45. If you watch the screen the whole day, you may become fatigued. So take breaks. Relax your eyes, take a nap in the afternoon, meditate, study market trends. Keep a diary.

46. Maintain energy levels to remain fearless and to make prompt decisions and executions.

DAILY SELF-AUDIT OF THE DAY'S TRADING

The trader should record every trading activity after the morning and afternoon session on a notepad in your smartphone.

1. How many trades in a day?

2. How long were you on screen in the morning and afternoon.

3. Did you trade based on well-informed decisions or were you impulsively influenced by free tips on TV channels?

4. More buy trades in the falling market will show your bias towards the bullish side. More sell trades in the gaining market indicate that you are a BEAR.

5. There will be huge losses after two days of profits.

6. One last trade without stoploss may have eroded all your profits.

7. See if you are making more profits by the end of the week in small equity trades instead of option trades.

You will learn the most from your own mistakes.

BIGGEST TRADING MISTAKES

1. **Whenever a stop goes off, it is wrong to trade within 10 minutes again**.

    If stoploss hits in the morning session around 10:00 a.m., then wait for the afternoon time slot at 2:00 p.m. If you suffer huge losses this month, wait for the next month for favourable opportunities. Try to recover losses in three parts. Sharpen your axe in the gap. Keep learning from your mistakes and study the market charts as well.

2. **It is a mistake to love or hate a stock or commodity scrip**.

    Don't make any trade in reaction to profit or loss. The right screener will suggest the right scrip for day trades. You can get rid of continuous reactions for any scrip.

    If you earn a lot of silver in two days, then do not touch it on the third day. When you consecutively earn 400 points for two days, on the third day you will reach 1200 points due to overconfidence.

3. **Whatever happens today, it will be the same tomorrow.**

    Do not believe this at all. Markets repeat their behaviour patterns, but it happens after such a long gap that most traders forget the patterns due to recency bias.

4. **It is dangerous to be occupied with the trading screen the entire day**.

    You can see things clearly from a distance only. If the trader sticks to the screen without breaks, then he will be trapped in the continuity of reactions. Profits will be eroded or stop losses will hit in dips or spikes when global market opens, or global data is disclosed.

5. **No tip or trial is free. Check the cost in your contract notes.**

Every beginner wants to see heaven without dying. But you will be ready to learn something only when you've been to HELL once. So, don't go for any readymade trading calls from advisors. Traders can try trading calls from reputed brokers for the purpose of learning.

If you get a call from any analyst, do not stick to the target. Buy on their advice, but book according to your capacity. Do not keep waiting till stop loss hits. You can reduce your position or create a hedge to have control in your hands.

6. **Chances of big profits come once a week.**

But keep booking small profits for daily gains. That is the real business. Take 1-1 runs. These will give you the power of sixes and fours. This means you must book small profits frequently. Every traditional business earns real profits in two months, but one must maintain the business for 10 of the 12 months preparing for those 2 REAL months.

7. **"It's not my real business. I'm doing it as a game only."**

This is a very dangerous approach. If you are involved in anything, you should try to learn the maximum about it. A single night of sex without a condom may cause AIDS or result in pregnancy. Online trading is a smart business, but if it is treated like a game, then it becomes very dangerous.

8. **How much will I earn daily?**

This is the most common question asked by an immature trader and fraud tippers give them dreamy profits of ₹25,000 per day. If you pay an extra ₹200 daily, then attempt to get back ₹300 daily first. If you try and test the services for one week after payment, then go for ₹1000 to ₹3000 daily.

9. **Nothing is running in the market?**

Every month, there may be a week which is totally range bound. You are paying the brokerage and gaining no profits at all. A mature trader passes this time without any big losses. If the market is not moving and you are not earning, then it is not your fault.

10. **I don't think that STOPLOSS will hit.**

What is the maximum amount I will lose if all my stocks hit SL? Ask yourself this before entering any trade. If the answer sounds scary, you will cut down volume to half. If you are ready for the worst-case scenario, then you will not react impulsively and double your losses. Stop if that negative or positive target is reached.

11. **I do not have internet connection.**

I trade over the phone only. I trade with an illegal broker, so micro lots are not allowed. You are not bound to all these reasons. The choice is always yours. You need not spend anything extra for the trading app on your smartphone and internet connection. If you calculate properly, you are losing the chance to gain ₹1000 extra daily.

12. **I have been trading for eight years, so I don't need any training.**

Trading is totally a knowledge-based business, and the market changes its behaviour every six months. So, a trader with 20 years of experience will get extra profits tomorrow, if he invests in extra knowledge today. Everyone makes patterns, regardless of what he does. One cannot see his own back. So, any mentor would be worthy to update even a PRO trader.

NIFTY MOVEMENT:

How, when and why it moves?

It is necessary to keep an eye on Nifty movements thoroughly.

1. If Nifty or the Sensex have been dipping for the last three days and you are planning to enter at bottom, but are too scared about a further fall, wait for one gap-up when the market opens. If the market is really witnessing a bullish reversal, the Sensex/Nifty will open with more than 0.5% gap-up and this too will run upside from there within 20 to 30 minutes.

2. If the Sensex/Nifty opens with less than 0.3% gap-up and you can buy index futures or stocks easily at a comfortable price, then it may be a false and unsustainable reversal.

   Jis gadi ko aasani se pakad Pao wo mostly chadne layak nhi. Chalo chadh bhi gye Josh me toh, Baithne layak toh hai hi nhi.

3. Nifty/Sensex will be range-bound after two days of clear movement on either side. So, reduce your trading volume or change instrument from futures to options or options to equity cash as per your risk capacity. Just wait for the next break out by placing high/low orders for the next five days.

4. Nifty/Sensex may run or fall for 7 to 10 days straight twice a year when they break yearly or are at an all-time high/low. Keep checking the three-month, one year and five-year charts occasionally. Traders lose maximum capital in such medium-term breakouts because they get trapped in the patterns of the last 3 to 4 months. When there was a positive breakout, they continued to short sell. Nifty was range bound from 10100 to 10800 for six months from February 18 to

November 18. When it broke 10800, many traders sold Nifty. It went to 11200 straight. Then they sold more to cost average and it went to 11700, erasing all their capital.

SECTOR WATCH IN THE STOCK MARKET

SHORT TO MEDIUM TERM SECTOR CYCLE OF THE STOCK MARKET GIVEN BELOW

You should pick a strong sector to buy and the weakest sector to sell. You can study sectors at bseindia.com or the index at nseindia.com. If you see the IT sector on top for the day, but if it has been on top for the past two to three days, then be careful. You should pick the second or third best sector, if they are moving from bottom to top for the day. In the same way, if realty hits bottom for the last two to three days, then choose the second last sector which moves from top to bottom. Use your common sense, which can be fine-tuned from regular observation. If you are trying to trade in OPTIONS (call-put), then choose the sectors in which options have regular good volumes. For example, the consumer durables sector is not good for option trading. If such sectors are strong, then choose cash trading or futures trading with strict minimum stoploss at the risk-free time slot. In the next posts, I will give you the list of stock options with good volumes. After a big move, either in the positive or negative direction for two days, there will be a rapid sector shuffling the following day. Top sectors hit bottom in an hour and the bottom sectors come on top. You may lose your trust in sector watch over these few days. But keep a regular watch of sectors before taking any decision.

How to decide the right Quantity, Stop loss and Target?

There shouldn't be one formula for stop loss and targets in changing market conditions. Try to practice minimum stop loss, because it is easy in recovery. If Nifty or any scrip has been going down for the last three to four days, then you can buy big volumes on reversal (say buy above VWAP or high that day). Expect big targets and keep a big stoploss at 2% to 5% after a day's reversal. The second day may show a big move if the reaction is still high. So keep buying above high with medium quantity, medium stoploss value and medium to large profits in parts because there may be profit booking on resistance levels. If Nifty or any scrip is on the pick after three days consecutive move, then buy minimum quantity with very small stoploss and quick profit booking with trailing stop losses. Sometimes, an unreasonable jump in price may be there, so you will be able to reap that huge profit.

Flexible targets for the stock market and mcx

Commodity online traders lose money most of the time due to rigid targets set by them or following random tips. For wise trading, one should have flexible targets. Keep tight control over stop losses because a loose stop loss system may be dangerous for capital protection. But targets are not that compulsory. Beginners should book small targets frequently. It will boost their confidence. If you see a profit in the beginning of trade and finally Stop Loss hits, then it is very frustrating for beginners. It may cause severe reactions. Generally, a trader should expect a little profit for 75% of the total time, because this will be range bound time. But for the remaining 25% of the time, one should attempt trailing stop losses for extraordinary profits. These special profits will fulfil the target at optimum levels. After any big downfall or gain (say 600 points in Nifty) a trader can expect a minimum of 200 to 300 points in short covering. If any stock or commodity falls by 15 to 25%, then expect 10% in a single shot another side. At all other times, plan for six points and get five points, then book it. Follow the trading time slots in the stock and mcx market. Book before 11:30 a.m. and re-enter after 1:30 p.m. and 3:10 p.m. for BTST in the stock market. Don't wait in the commodities mcx for more than 20 to 30 minutes. You may re-enter in the next time slot, but don't wait till stoploss hits.

LOGIC has its limits, so take a simple leap of faith in day trading in the stock market and commodity mcx

When we do comprehensive technical analysis and there is a lot of data available, so many traders face the same problems. The problem is to choose or pick any scrip or method to go ahead. Most traders become confused after seeing so many options and avoid making any decisions.

You see any screener which lists hundreds of stocks; how do you choose two or three of them? Here you need a simple approach. Just pick any two shares having a price greater than ₹500 and observe their behaviour in the coming days. You can't avoid mistakes totally in the beginning, but do not avoid action at all. So you need to take a leap of faith after considering the many screeners and technical indicators. One can observe good; he may analyse well too but one important part remains and that is to conclude. Learn to conclude without unreasonable fear. What will be the maximum?

FUTURES & OPTIONS (EQUITY DERIVATIVES)

Futures and Options are a comparatively new system of trading. There are chances of huge profits and losses because it involves trading in lots (huge scale). There are different types of futures. One is Index futures. There are various kinds of index futures. **Nifty and bank Nifty** futures are the most popular index futures. We can trade in international indices as well. We have Stock futures. There are many kinds of stock futures. It started with 18 futures. Today, there are 500 to 600 futures. Lot sizes are fixed by exchanges in such a manner that the value of each future remains within ₹4 to ₹6 lacs. So if the stock price is ₹20, then the lot size may be around 25,000, so the value will be ₹5 lacs. If the stock price is ₹4000, then the lot size may be around 150, so the value is ₹6 lacs. We can buy any future by paying a 10 to 20% margin and holding the position till expiry. Traders can google search for NSE futures lot sizes and margins; they will find many websites with daily updates of stock futures.

Why were futures needed?

The main reason was the limitation of the total quantity of any stock. So if there is some good news about a certain stock, traders buy 500 crore shares in delivery and wait for the same. But if the total number of stocks issued are 300 crores, then the stocks will not be delivered in the demat account of so many traders. That's why futures were introduced. These are imaginary bundles of stocks. So there is no limitation of quantity. It is like 22 players are playing cricket on the ground, but lacs of players are playing outside the ground, betting on the game being played. It is like a derivative.

Benefits of futures

1. Less capital required. A 10 to 20% margin is okay to enter trade.

2. Lower brokerage cost. There is no brokerage cost for delivery because no actual delivery process is required.

3. Positional short selling is possible. You have to square off the short-sold position in intraday till 3:30 p.m. or the stocks will go on auction and you will have to pay a penalty. But you can short sell any future for 10 days, one month or two months and wait for the downfall. It gives you the opportunity to hedge your position in the cash market or future itself. So, you are safe in any overnight crisis.

4. Trading in INDEX (Nifty/Bank Nifty) is possible due to futures trading only. Nifty has the maximum turnover in futures. It is difficult to choose the right sector and stock, but the index trade will give you a simple and single-minded approach.

Drawbacks of futures and options

1. If you buy a single stock of any company, then you become an official partner of said company. They will treat you like a partner. You will be sent reports, invitation to meetings and asked for your vote in making big decisions. But if you buy a lot of 1000 shares in futures, you won't have any involvement in the company.

2. Immature traders make huge positions due to the margin facility. When they suffer huge losses, they cost average their position due to the pressure of losses. And this may create huge, unaffordable losses. If someone doesn't have the ability to afford losses, then he will try anything to cover his losses. If someone has the capacity to suffer losses, then he will accept them and think with a cool mind. The last Thursday of the month is when the futures and options expire. Futures price is not the same as the cash market price. If the futures price is more than the underlying, then it is called futures at a premium. If the futures price is less than the underlying, then the futures is at a discount. There are three series available in futures.

This month: Running month is December. If one buys this month, then he can wait till the last Thursday of this month or he can sell within five minutes if he wants to.

Next month: January. If one buys next month, he can wait till expiry of the next month, but he may be able to buy or sell January futures in December anytime.

Far month: February. There may be a little difference in price in all these series, but the relative movement is not much different.

ROLLOVER

If you suffer losses in this month's futures and hope to recover next month, then you can sell this month and buy next month futures. This is ROLLOVER.

Rollover is not feasible in options, because the difference in their premium may be more than 100 to 200%. One should start trading practice in the cash market first with low volume, then increase the volume gradually in cash. It will give you proper insight about stock behaviours. The index options/index futures and stock options will be the next stage. Stock futures should be the final stage only if it is affordable and is needed.

What are OPTIONS and why are they needed?

Nifty futures is around ₹9 lacs in value and needs a 10 to 20% margin only (may be 80k). If someone doesn't have this kind of money, there are other instruments available with minimum capital requirements and limited losses. It is not possible to have uncontrolled huge losses in OPTIONS like futures. If you think there is a possibility of 100 points upside in Nifty futures and you don't have the margin to trade in futures or you don't want to take such a big risk, you can BUY CALL (Nifty) instead of buying nifty futures. There are different strike prices available. Suppose nifty is at 17,900 now. So, 17,900, 18,000, 18,100, and 18,200 strike prices are available, which can have a decreasing premium with distant strike price. Strike price is NOT price. PREMIUM is the price you pay. Actual price is 100, 80, 60 and 40. If lot size of Nifty is 50, then the price for the above-mentioned calls will be Rs 100*50 = 5000 / 80*50 = 4000 / 60*50 = 3000 / 40*50 = 2000. Margin trading is not allowed in OPTIONS. One should have the complete amount in his trading account to buy options.

PUTS are traded in the downward direction, so the strike price of 17,900, 17,800, 17,700 and 17,600 will have a decreasing premium:100, 80, 60, 40. The price for the above mentioned PUTS will be Rs 100*50 = 5000 / 80*50 = 4000 / 60*50 = 4000 / 40*50 = 2000.

There are 3 types of OPTIONS based on the strike price.

ATM: At the MONEY call/put. If Nifty runs at 17,900, then 17,900 call and put are AT the money (ATM call/put).

In the money-ITM call/PUT. If nifty is at 17,900, then it has already passed 17800, 17700 and 17600 in the case of CALLS. All these calls are in the money calls. If Nifty is 17,900, then it has already passed 18000, 18100 and 18200 in the case of PUTS. All these PUTS are in the money PUTS.

You can see the OPTION CHAIN on the right upper corner of any page on NSEindia.com. The upper left part in light-yellow shade shows the money calls and the lower right part shows In the money puts. The option chain doesn't show open, high, low and close of any call/put (option). You should go to the back page and then GET the **derivative quote** from the same upper right corner of the page about any stock.

OTM call/put (Out of money)

These calls are yet to come. Suppose Reliance Industries is at 2200. Then for CALLS, 2220, 2240, 2260 and 2280 strike prices are yet to come. For PUTS, 2180, 2160, 82140 and 2120 strike prices are yet to come. Option positional trades are safe in the beginning of the month. It is risky to buy call/put in the third and fourth (expiry) week. However, short selling of call/put may be better in the third or fourth week. OTM calls and puts show maximum time decay and reduce to almost zero on the expiry day.

Option price is made up of intrinsic value + time value

All index options (NIFTY/Bank Nifty call/put) have WEEKLY EXPIRY every Thursday. Stock options and all FUTURES have monthly expiry on the LAST THURSDAY of the month. Time value of an option reduces gradually, day by day, near expiry. So, all out of money calls and puts may reduce to almost zero premium on the expiry date due to time decay. Observe the equity derivatives in the live market on nseindia.com. You will see Nifty futures and Nifty options on the first page with top turnover. On the left side, there is a view box which will show the top 20 stock futures and top 20 stock options. See monthly top gainers and losers of Nifty, Nifty next 50 and Nifty midcap. Keep daily records of these: 3 gainer stocks, 3 loser stocks, Nifty, bank Nifty, at the money and most active calls/puts. Observe the changing behaviours with Nifty and sector movement.

HEDGING

(Protecting capital in UPS and DOWNS)

HEDGING means protecting capital during sudden reversals of market. For example, if you bought Drreddy in dip at ₹3000 and there is a risk of a further dip, you can buy Drreddy futures with put (3000 strike price). If you buy 20/50 shares in cash only, then a small put with a lower premium is enough (2500/2700 strike price). Hedging may be possible in many ways.

1. Buy future + buy put

2. Sell future + buy call

3. Buy future December + sell future in January with small stoploss on both sides. This is called Calendar spread.

4. Buy most active call + put

5. Sell far out of money CALL + PUT with strict stop loss in the third or fourth week. Writing calls and puts have unlimited losses. If you buy call/put at ₹100 premium, then it may reduce to zero.

If you sell call/put at ₹100, then it may go to 400/600/1000 or higher.

So unlimited losses are possible.

SYMBOL FOR INSTRUMENT TYPE (FUTURES & OPTIONS)

- **FUTIDX** – Index futures (Nifty/bank Nifty futures)
- **OPTIDX** – Index options (Nifty/bank Nifty CALL/PUT)
- **OPTSTK** – Stock options (acc to zeel CALL/PUT)
- **FUTSTK** – Stock futures (around 500 + futures available)

  All stock and index options don't have regular volume.

  There are 40 to 50 stock options that have regular volume.

  How can you recognize less volume options?

  The option chain is blank in most parts.

  There is a big difference in ask and bid price.

WHY AND HOW TO TRADE IN STOCK

OPTION (CALL/PUT)?

Option was not well understood or a misunderstood instrument in the Indian stock market. But it is the best solution for both small and big traders. Options involve limited risk. If you see bullishness in say the Reliance Industries at 850, you expect it to go up to 920 in 10 days. Now, there are many ways to trade this opportunity. First, buy 100 RIL shares. Invest 85,000 + 1.5% in delivery brokerage and taxes. Profits may be more than ₹7000. Second, trade intraday daily, but it may be difficult to get 30 points out of the total 70 point movement, because the market gives the biggest chunk of profit in the GAP UP opening. All day traders miss this chance. But their cost is maximum in terms of time, energy and daily brokerage, even if intraday brokerage is 0.1% only. Third, buy 1 call option. Suppose price (premium) of 900 call is 20, then investment is 20*250 = 5000 total so, our maximum risk is ₹5000 only and the profit, unlimited. Trading costs (brokerage + taxes) is around ₹100 per trade. If the direction is not clear, and you are unsure whether RIL will go up or down, then buy call for bull trend + buy PUT for bear trend. Total investment is ₹5000 for CALL and ₹5000 for PUT. Sometimes, I have seen up to ₹50,000 in profits for this investment of ₹10,000, when Nifty breaks its medium-term levels. Generally, ₹5000 can be gained with an investment of ₹10,000. Make a safe combo and sleep for 10 days till the 15th of the month. The last Thursday is the expiry date. CALL/PUT show prices decay near expiry. You should not make any CALL/PUT combination without a specific reason. If the market goes up or down suddenly, then you will profit. If the stock becomes range bound, then both CALL and PUT premiums will decrease due to time decay, causing losses. If RIL goes up to ₹920 from ₹850, then you will profit anywhere between ₹5000 and ₹7000 with an investment and risk of ₹5000 only.

SMALL PROFITS, FREQUENTLY

Jobbing or scalping in online day trading

When any trader enters and exits a trade with speed and gets small profits frequently, he rarely repents and earns well. But he should have time discipline and make decisions based on sound technical analysis. If you trade at any time without enough reason to buy or sell, then you will be over trading, which is not suggested. In any type of online trading, may it be mcx, stock market or currency, this trick is useful for big and small traders. Many people enter into the trade after two small profits. They become greedy or overconfident. They hope to make huge profits in a single shot without stop loss or with a big stop loss. In any other traditional business, you face so many people a day. All don't become your clients. Some of them give you negligible volumes and margins. But a few give you huge margins, which can justify your daily targets. In case of commodity trading, you may trade in silver three to six times a day, perhaps at 10:54 a.m., 2:29 p.m., 4:29 p.m., 5:54 p.m., 6:54 p.m. and 7:30 p.m. (See detailed time slots in another post.) For more than six times, you took stoploss of 100 points. Three times you hit stop loss, you lose $100*3 = 300$ points. Twos times you make a very small profit: $200*2 = 400$ points. Once you definitely make a big profit = 400 points, so the net profit is − $300+400+400 = +500$ points. The same is applicable for crude, copper or NG or any other commodity. In the same stop loss and at the same time (five to 10 minutes) you can earn big profits because the market moves in waves. So there is no regular movement. You can observe this fact in any chart of any commodity. So, what is the right strategy? Begin trading when there are enough reasons. Apply very strict stop loss each time and exit within three to 10 minutes. (Sometimes, it may be cost to cost.) Do not wait to hit SL after a given time slot because hitting stop losses creates a mental imbalance in the trader, which disturbs the whole day's trading. When you have less wickets in hand (small capital), then it is wise to take single runs until you reach a good score. Sixes and fours will come in obviously after that. With the same system, there are jobbing desks, where so many salaried traders enter into a trade for multiple lots and book profit within minutes. Many big companies handle the trading accounts of international HNI clients.

Option Greeks

It is important for the active option trader to become familiar with Delta, Gamma, Theta, and Vega characteristics, since he may need to make quick decisions about trading strategies and risk management, decisions which might well determine his financial fate. The following is a summary of these characteristics:

Delta

Deltas range from zero for far out-of-the-money calls to 100 for deeply in-the-money calls, and from zero for out-of-the-money puts to 100 for deeply in-the-money puts. At-the-money calls have Deltas of approximately 50, and at-the-money puts, approximately 50. As time passes, or as you decrease your volatility assumption, call Deltas move away from 50, and put Deltas away from 50. As you increase your volatility assumption, call Deltas move towards 50, and put Deltas towards 50.

Gamma

At-the-money options have greater Gammas than either in or out-the-money options with otherwise identical contract specifications. As you increase your volatility assumption, the Gamma of an in or out-of-the-money option rises, while the Gamma of an at-the-money option falls. As you decrease your volatility assumption, or as the time to expiration nears, the Gamma of an in or out-of-the-money option falls, while the Gamma of an at-the-money option rises, sometimes dramatically.

Theta

At-the-money options have greater Thetas than either in or out-of-the-money options with otherwise identical contract specifications. The Theta of an at-the-money option increases as the expiration date approaches. A short-term, at-the-money option will always decay more quickly than a long-term, at-the-money option. As you increase your volatility assumption, the Theta of an option will rise. Higher volatility means there is greater time value associated with the option, so that each day's decay will also be greater when no movement occurs.

Vega

At-the-money options have greater Vegas than either in or out-of-the-money options with otherwise identical contract specifications. Out-of-the-money options have the greatest Vega as a percent of theoretical value. The Vegas of all options decrease as time to expiration grows shorter. A long-term option is always more sensitive to a change in volatility than a short-term option with otherwise identical contract specifications. The Vega of an at-the-money option is relatively constant with respect to changes in volatility. If you raise or lower volatility, the option's Vega is unlikely to change significantly.

Various strategies for options trading

1. Long call – bullish (less capital equal to premium only)

2. Short call – limited profit, much capital needed

3. Synthetic long call – buy stock / buy put.

4. Long put – bearish

5. Short put – limited profits, unlimited losses

6. Covered call – buy stock – sell call of buy

7. Long combo – sell a put, buy a call

8. Synthetic long put – sell stock + buy call

9. Covered put = sell stock + sell put

10. Buy put + buy call = long straddle

11. Sell put + sell call = short straddle

12. Buy otm put + buy otm call = long strangle

    (less cost but big move needed).

13. Sell otm put + sell otm call = short strangle

14. Buy stock + buy put + sell call = collar

    RIL fut at 2200 – buy 2180 put + sell 2260 call

15. Bull call spread buy 17500 call + sell 17700

    Buy itm call + sell otm call

16. Bull put spread sell OTM, buy lower strike put,

    sell 17500 put, buy 17300.

17. Bear call spread sell 17600 + buy 17500,

    sell lower strike call + buy otm call

18. Bear put spread buy itm put + sell otm put

    Buy 17700 put + sell 17500

10 mistakes of options trading

1. Without hedging (guessing direction)

2. Carry intraday to positional

3. Start directly with stock options instead of knowing underlying stock behaviour with equity cash.

4. Next trade just after booking profit.

5. Jump in option volume after profits or losses, not knowing the complex, weekly changing options behaviours.

6. Concluding a formula with limited observations.

7. Getting confused between index and stock options.

8. Not setting profit goals and limits on losses.

9. Paying huge fees in unexpected losses before actual training.

10. Following random tips even after losing capital many times.

Bank nifty call put re balancing

Suppose you bought bank Nifty options long strangle before some big event or after a long tight range. You buy 31500 call in ₹300 premium. You buy 31000 put in ₹300 premium. The total investment is 600 points*lot size 25 = 15,000. You are ready here for any big movement on either side. Now the bank Nifty moves from 31,200 to 31,500 due to some positive trigger. So call premium has increased by 300 to 520. Put premium has reduced by 300 to 120. The total is 520 + 120 = 640 now.

I expect bank Nifty to go from 32,000 to 33,000 from today, levelling at 31,500 in the near future. But there will be profit booking after every upside move. So, if there is a technical correction of 150 to 300 points only (0.5 to 1%), what will happen? The call will reduce by 50 to 60% (520 to 230). Put will increase by 50 to 70% (130 to 200), because now the put has become far out of money. So the total is 200 + 230 = 430 now, 210 points less than the previous day's total.

We need to re balance the position. So, sell that long strangle, both calls put in 640. And buy a new combination with the latest perspective. So, there's a bull run in bank Nifty for the last three days. So, selling is expected more than further buying. You can buy a bigger put with a smaller OTM call now. So, at 31500, you bought 31,400 put at ₹250 premium and bought 31,800 call at ₹200 premium.

If there is a 200 point downfall, put may rise from 250 to 380 and call may dip from 200 to 120.

Now, the total is 500. You can sell the combo and rebalance again.

Calls and puts are chosen on the basis of the premium, not the strike price.

If you follow the last five days highs/lows and mid-day breakout strategy daily, parallel to such long strangles, you will be safe in any sudden reversal.

TRADING OPERATIONS (ODIN DETAILS)

You can start your trading account with any private broker or bank. Go to google.com and search for a commodity/stock national or international market broker in your location. You just fill in the inquiry form and they will come to your residence to complete further formalities. You must find a broker who can Email or WhatsApp forms and documents to be signed by you. Your address and ID proof, photographs, bank details, a cancelled cheque and pan card will be required for this. The process to open an account will take two to five days to complete. The broker will load the trading software on to your computer. You can trade on your own if you download the trading application or you can trade over the phone by calling your operator at the broker's office. ODIN is the most popular trading software used in the Indian market. Some very essential operations will be explained here.

Select any commodity or stock, then press **F1 for buy order.** You can enter LIMIT PRICE or MARKET PRICE to buy or sell. After buying **put SL by pressing the F2 key, SELL ORDER** for STOPLOSS. You will have to enter TRIGGER PRICE and LIMIT PRICE. Press **F2 for SELL order** PUT STOPLOSS and F1 for buy order. **F3-F3 TO SEE ORDER BOOK.** You can change or cancel any pending order from this list. Press **F5 to see buyers and sellers, open, high, low, close and weighted average. ALT+F6** to see integrated position quantity, profits or losses. You can sell or buy your holdings directly from here only. **Double-click F8 to see all trades that you've** already executed. (Pending orders are not shown here.) You can list any commodity on the screen and form your own market watch. You can list the index on the upper right corner of the screen. Call to discuss the details or if you have any confusion.

NEAT SCREEN

There are many trading software applications. The most popular are ODIN by Finantech and neat/NOW by nse/BOLT (bse). This is the mother software which brokers customise to suit their needs. The trader workstation screen is divided into the following windows:

1. **Title bar:**

    It displays the trading system name i.e., NEAT, the trading member's name, the user ID, user type, the date and the current time.

2. **Ticker window:**

    The ticker displays information of all trades in the system as and when it takes place. The user has the option of selecting the securities that should appear in the ticker.

3. **Tool bar:**

    The toolbar has functional buttons which can be used with the mouse for quick access to various functions such as buy order entry, sell order entry, market by price (MBP), previous trades (PT), outstanding order (OO), activity log (AL), order status (OS), market watch (MW), snap quote (SQ) and market movement (MM).

4. **Market watch window:**

    The market watch window is the main area of focus for a trading member. This screen allows continuous monitoring of the securities that are of specific interest to the user. It displays trading information for the selected securities.

5. **Inquiry window:**

    This screen enables the user to view information such as market by order (MBO), market by price (MBP), previous trades (PT), outstanding orders (OO), activity log (AL), order status (OS), market movement (MM), market inquiry (MI), net position, online backup, index inquiry, indices broadcast, most active securities and so on.

6. **Snap quote:**

The snap quote feature allows a trading member to get instantaneous market information on any desired security. This is normally used for securities that are not already set in the market watch window.

7. **Order/trade window:**

This window enables the user to enter/modify/cancel orders and to send requests for trade cancellations and modifications.

8. **Message window:**

This enables the user to view messages broadcast by the exchange such as corporate actions, any market news, auctions related information, etc.

MARKET WATCH for the stock market.

Your market watch is like LAND for money farming. Take care of this daily. Make a special market watch daily from 3:25 p.m., all in one screener of monthly/yearly breakout stocks and short-term breakouts from chartink.

1. For the stock market, see nseindia.com and the top two gainers and top two losers from Nifty, Nifty next 50 and midcap. List them all daily from 9:30 to 9:40 a.m.

2. Nifty futures /bank Nifty futures may be placed at the top.

3. Keep A group stocks only in the market watch so that a beginner won't be trapped in low quality stocks.

4. Be conscious of stocks with similar names and those that are similarly priced. It may lead to mistakes many times.

5. Keep rearranging the market watch daily because it will include new stocks with hourly updated day trading screeners.

6. Include some stocks from the main screeners like volume increase, price rise, recovery from intraday low and gap up opening.

7. If you can manage another portfolio for options then make a new scrip portfolio (market watch) for them. Otherwise, the lower part of the screen may be used for options of top gainers and loser stocks from Nifty/midcap.

Warren Buffet once said that old data is quite an EYE OPENER. So, keep watching historical charts and prices of nifty100/BSE500 constituents.

FUTURE strategy (Monthly Plan)

First week:

Buy nifty fut + buy put / sell Nifty fut + buy call (same in bank Nifty). Stock future buys above high in strong sector (last month's loser.) Sell below Low in weak sector (last month's gainers).

Second week:

(More focus on options) Collar strategy: Buy nifty future + buy put + sell call

Sell nifty future + buy call + sell put

Same in bank nifty and monthly gainer / loser stocks.

One future is hedged by two options here.

Third week:

Sell Nifty November + buy Nifty December at 9:54 a.m. or 1:54 p.m. sl – 8p Tgt 14p.

Sell bank Nifty November + buy bank Nifty December at 9:54 a.m. or 1:54 p.m., sl 30pt, TGT 60pt.

Buy at high + sell at low in Gainer/Loser stocks, hedging with SELL call in buying.

SELL put with selling and strict stop loss in future.

Fourth week:

Buy at high + sell at low in index futures and stock futures. Book fast within five minutes.

TECHNICAL ANALYSIS

There are two types of analysis in the commodity/stock market or any screen based trading market like currency-forex.

1. **FUNDAMENTAL ANALYSIS**: It tells us WHAT to buy/sell. It depends on the actual demand and supply. It will discuss production, demand, inventory and government policies. Main tools used in this analysis are data and facts. It mainly helps to understand the short term or positional move in the coming months and years. It is more complicated, time consuming and considered less useful in day trading. But if you are picking intraday stocks with very strong fundamentals, then RISK/reward Ratio will be highest because MF and FII focus on such stocks.

2. **TECHNICAL ANALYSIS**: It tells us WHEN to buy/sell. It depends on buyers and sellers who are more affected by recent sentiments instead of actual demand and supply. The main tools are CHARTS which show movement of price and volume with time. The main types of charts are:

LINE chart

Line chart shows the UPTREND when the line is going up. Downtrend is depicted by the RED line. When the price neither goes up nor down and is bound in range, it is called SIDEWAYS.

Candlestick chart

Candlestick shows minute to minute details of movement. Green or white colour shows the upside. RED or black shows the downside. There are so many candlestick patterns to understand the periodical behaviour of any scrip. How to practice candlestick when investing. See the three-month and one-year chart, then click on the double arrows opposite the candlestick. Read three-star high reliable patterns first, followed by the medium and low reliable ones. See direction and volume first with three-month and one-year chart. Then move on to weekly and daily duration. See the candlestick pattern formation shown by the letter P. Click it to see the name and reliability. Area charts and Bar charts are not very useful for trading purposes.

There are **3 main trends** in a chart:

Uptrend – When the price moves upside clearly due to strong buying and the price makes the pick.

Downtrend – When price falls downside clearly due to strong selling and makes bottom.

Sideways or range bound – When there is no positive or negative trigger, then buyers and sellers become indecisive and the stock price becomes range-bound.

RESISTANCE – is the price where the uptrend stops due to profit booking and the price falls. There are many resistance levels in various charts (daily/monthly/decade) R1-R2-up breakout.

SUPPORT – is the price where the downtrend stops due to fresh buying or short covering and the price goes up accordingly. There are many support levels in various charts (intraday or historical) S1-S2 – down breakout.

BOLLINGER BAND

It shows the recent highs and lows. There are three bands. The central band is 30 days dma. The upper band is central band + 2 sigma. The lower band is 30 dma (central band) – 2*sigma. Sigma is the standard deviation. This is the average of 30-day ranges, while 30 dma is the average of 30-day closing price.

If the stock price touches the upper band, then keep selling at the weekly low. If CMP of the stock touches the lower band, then keep buying at the weekly high.

There are **4 types** of technical indicators:

1. Trend
2. Momentum
3. Volatility
4. Volume indicators.

Trend indicators

These technical indicators show change of trends.

Moving Averages: 200 dma and 50 dma are the most important. Golden cross is a good technical indicator. Use trendlyne screener for Nifty 200 shares to find golden crossover stocks.

AROON: Aroon up line for uptrend. Aroon down line for downtrend.

Parabolic Stop and Reverse (Parabolic SAR): Finds reversals in the market price.

Average Directional Index (ADX): Negative adx shows the selling trends. A positive ADX shows a bullish or buying trend.

Moving Average Convergence Divergence (MACD): When slow line (9 dma) goes above the fast line (12 to 26 dma), then it is time to SELL.

Momentum indicators

These technical indicators may identify the speed of price movements by comparing the current closing price to previous closes.

Stochastic Oscillator / William% R: Used to predict price turning points by comparing the closing price to its price range.

Commodity Channel Index (CCI): An oscillator that identifies price reversals, price extremes, and trend strength.

Relative Strength Index (RSI): Scrip prices moves between 30 to 70 levels when tracked for the last 14 trading days. If it touches 70, then it is OVERBOUGHT. When it touches 30, it is OVERSOLD.

Volatility Indicators

These indicators measure the rate of price movement in either direction.

Bollinger bands / Donchain : Checks stocks near monthly support for potential BUY in the forthcoming days. Checks stocks near monthly resistance for SELL.

Average True Range: Shows price volatility.

Volume Indicators

These indicators tell the strength of a trend on volume of shares traded.

Chaikin Oscillator: Shows the flow of money in and out of the market, which happens on tops and bottoms.

On-Balance Volume (OBV): Level of accumulation or distribution, by comparing volume to price.

Volume Rate of Change (ROC): Highlights increase in volume. This happens mostly at market tops, bottoms, or breakouts.

TRADING TUNNEL THEORY – LOWER/UPPER CIRCUIT STRATEGY

What to do when any commodity slips in the lower or upper circuit? Suppose silver falls by 4% in the afternoon, then goes further down by 6%. Many traders who have been waiting to buy for days, buy silver on the first fall (at 1000 points but it falls further by 2300 points.) All traders feel totally trapped. Do not have any prior assumptions to BUY or SELL any stock or commodity. Do what the chart-buyer and average shows. So, if silver does not rise above AVERAGE, there are three to four times as many sellers. So keep selling it on every jump. At 4% or 6% you must open hedging on both sides with strict STOPLOSS. If you follow a single direction, i.e. BUYING and hit SL two to three times, you won't dare to buy again at the right time. If you are in single side SELLING mode with a small SL (50 points in gold) and SL hits, it bounces up by 400 points. Then, you won't lose 50 points only. But you will have the rare opportunity of 400 plus points. So, think of HEDGING positively, even if it does not give you profits five times out of 10.

SOME IMPORTANT TECHNICAL RULES

1. If any share or commodity has been falling freely over the last two days, on the third day, it jumps up a little and breaks that day's low again, making way for the biggest downfall. Many traders get trapped in buying without stoploss, because they assume that the commodity won't go down very much after a two-day fall.

2. Same case is applicable after two days of huge buying. Use DOUBLE STOPLOSS STRATEGY in both the above cases.

3. If any stock shows a crossover like – 2% to +2% then you MUST buy with strict stoploss. If any commodity crosses – 0.5% and + 0.5% buy it with 0.3% stoploss in the next dip. On August 2, silver moved 1200 points from – 1.5% to +1.5%.

4. After breaking any high or low stock or commodity take a breather. So buy/sell in a dip. If there's no dip, buy or sell mini volumes (say 2kg silver instead of 5kg).

5. After three days of a continuous fall, try buying two to three times with medium stoploss and medium volume. After a three-day rally, buy with caution on picks with very small stoploss and low volume.

6. Study all the rules and get ready with STOPLOSS LIMIT orders already on moves. No tipper gets time to send the tip in a sudden sharp bounce.

7. After two days of clear moves, there will be two days of rangebound movement so don't sell anything by guessing picks, or buy in a hurry, guessing the bottom.

8. A real big move starts when maximum traders are already exhausted.

9. Avoid the stock or commodity that has confusing parameters. Focus on the commodity which has clear parameters.

HOW TO USE SIMPLE MOVING AVERAGE (SMA) IN MCX/ NIFTY TRADING?

SIMPLE MOVING AVERAGE (SMA)

If you add three days closing price of any scrip and divide it by three, you will get the simple moving average. If you take the average of the first, second and third of July, then in the next moving average, remove July 1 and take the closing price of July 2, 3 and 4. I've explained the three-day moving average for convenience, but generally 30 DMA, 50 DMA and 200 DMA are very popular. You don't have to calculate these averages; already calculated DMAs are available on many websites. It helps us understand the trend of any scrip. If the price chart of any scrip crosses 30 or 50 DMA and continues to go up, then a new short-term buying trend will have started and will sustain. This is called a bullish crossover. If it goes down, then a short-term selling trend is confirmed. This is a bearish crossover. When 200 DMA crossover is there, it may be medium term. In the above chart, we can see clearly that the blue line (50 DMA) has crossed the red line (200 DMA) and has gone further down. This signifies a big selling trend. When the blue line crosses the red line goes up, this signifies a big buying trend, and it will be sustained above that level.

MACD – MOVING AVERAGE convergence and divergence works on a similar concept but I won't get into this to keep things simple. Decisions should be firm but prompt.

TECHNICAL ANALYSIS – TRENDLINE

TRENDLINE is a line made by joining picks (highs) made in a price chart or by joining bottoms (lows).

RESISTANCE: When the price of any scrip can't go up above a certain level, then it is called resistance. It happens due to big selling forces on a particular price. A scrip has various resistance levels for a period. Say, silver is at cmp 40, 200 then R1 – 40450, R2 – 40680, R3 – 40860. R3 can be considered the OVERBOUGHT level, where fresh buying may be risky.

SUPPORT: When the price of any scrip can't go down below a certain level, then it is called support. In the above given example of silver, S1 may be 40250, S2 40030 and S3 39880. S3 can be considered the OVERSOLD level, where fresh selling may be risky.

When any commodity falls by 6% and short sellers book their profit, then the price may bounce by 1 to 2%. The price can't be stable here. It goes down again. This buying is called SHORTCOVERING.

What is fresh buying/selling?

If FRESH BUYING happens, then the price becomes stable. It may break the previous high. In the figure given below, the TRENDLINE'S blue part works like a support and the red part is like resistance. In the INTRADAY timeframe, when you see any commodity chart by pressing the ctrl+I key, notice if any strong support breaks at the time of data (2:30 to 8:30 p.m.). This will become very strong resistance. STRONG support or resistance means that the price chart may touch that line and reverse back three to four times.

So, with the above trendline, buy on every dip near the trendline and keep the stop losses below the trendline (blue arrows shown in figure). Below the trendline, sell on every jump near the trendline and keep the stop losses above the trendline (red arrows shown in the figure).

HOMEWORK: Notice the following day on screen, if any commodity is in buying, it's average will improve every hour. It means the ATP of NG was 222.5, then it becomes 222.9 and 223.4. This confirms strong buying. In the case of selling, the ATP goes below every hour.

How to use SIMPLE MOVING AVERAGE (SMA) in mcx commodity trading?

We can trade maximum with minimum risk if we learn to trade with minimal stoploss or micro SL (0.1 to 0.2%). If we take 0.2% SL for five times or 0.1% for 10 times, then it will total 1%. Will such small stop losses work for profit? If SL hits seven out of 10 times, then the calculation will be 0.1*7 = 0.7% losses. Profits will be 0.4*3 = 1.2%, because we have limited the losses, not the profits. Profits will always be higher. Bargain first for minimum brokerage fees with your broker. It will support this plan. See the chart from 10:00 a.m. to 10:00 p.m. for three days. Observe minutely all the timings of movements and percentages of movements. When you look at the NG chart as of 12/08/2013, it opened in plus. There was a big downfall over the last three trading days, but a positive reversal was there on that day. You can see the moves at 10:30 a.m., 11:10a.m., 1:00 p.m. and finally 2:30 p.m. Before 2:30 p.m., it was positive, but below ATP. So the movement was small and within a range. Levels touched in the chart were 197, 197.5, 198, 198.5, and 199. So, it was 198 at 10:30 a.m. Place buying defensive at 197.5 SL 197.2, TGT may be between 198 and 198.5 (more than double the SL). At 1:00 p.m. it reached a high of 199.2. You sold at 198.5. SL 198.8. (If you hit SL, sell again at 199, SL 199.3. This time it was close to the SL but did not hit it and slipped to 197.6. You can book 1 point out of a 1.7 point move. At 2:30 p.m., it finally crossed its ATP in a sudden sharp move. If you got a 1 point profit, then it is easy to repeat 0.3 SL again. The chart shows a clear support level at 197.6. Suppose you bought at 197.7, SL 197.4 or 198 SL 197.7 (you can use multiple buy trades at such levels with 0.3 SL, detailed in the earlier blogpost). It crossed the ATP of 198.4 and touched 199. It is possible to add one to two more lots on such crossovers with a 30 point sl. It didn't come down and touched 200-200.8.

The most promising timings as per my observation: Use 0.3 SL four times before 2:30 p.m. dip, 4:30 p.m., 6:30 p.m. and 7:30 p.m. You can change these timings according to your observations on trend changing days. It's not possible to catch every profitable move. You will miss 50% of them. But do not repent or react, even if you are able to make 50% of the trades. It will double your daily target. The reason is that you target five trades; three trades will create no profit, no losses or 0.5 losses. Your fourth trade will give you a small profit. One out of five will give you 1.5 to 3 points straight and your targets will be met. If you add one to two lots on crossover, then the profits may be five to six points.

PART – II

DOUBLE STOPLOSS STRATEGY IN INTRADAY/ ONLINE TRADING

DOUBLE STOPLOSS STRATEGY

Whenever there is a big down fall in the market or lower circuits, the trader is in great confusion. Rates seem very attractive. The trader buys two to three times but SL hits all the time. Anyone may consider doing without the SL just once and gets trapped in a 2000 point loss in a single evening. When silver or gold becomes weak, then sell it with strict stoploss. But what about the REVERSAL which happens on every pick or bottom? If you sell only in bottom, then a stoploss of 200 to 300 points will hit in bounce back. The trader will not lose this 200 to 300 points at this time, but he will lose this rare opportunity to gain 1500 to 2000 points in a bounce back. With the DOUBLE STOPLOSS METHOD, if silver is at 40,300 (-2.5%) and the average is 40,500, then sell one lot at 40,300 and keep the stoploss of two lots above the 40,500 average. If there is a bounce back of 800 points, then 200 points will go in the stoploss and you have a 600-point profit. This method is useful, especially in extreme picks and valleys (bottom). A trader does not lose due to lack of technical knowledge. He incurs losses due to lack of common sense which comes from regular observation, identifying mistakes and not repeating them.

A trader starts trading very lightly. He makes a profit by chance. It happens because he is fearless in the beginning. When he earns ₹3000 in a day, he simply calculates 25*3000 = 75,000 monthly income. He earns more than the planned profits in the first week. He becomes confident and fearless. It is hard for him to understand what the problem is in trading with old traders? Then, suddenly, the market reverses and shows its quarterly stormy movements, which are unpredictable and have been miscalculated by this new trader. He loses more than all his profits earned in the past weeks in just three days. Still, he hopes to get lucky, but a deep fear is planted within. If he had lost ₹1 lac, then he wants to recover this ₹1 lac in the next week. He tries some good tips and earns ₹15,000 in two days with big lots trading. He develops a blind trust in the tipper and decides to go for four big lots in one shot. A very good tipper may have the chance to hit SL once a week. So, the trader loses Rs 40,000 in a single stoploss. He blames his destiny but common sense says that after two days of making good profits, he should have reduced his targets, since that scrip will be volatile and rangebound due to profit-booking pressure. After every loss, he either blames all the others around him (his tipper, operator, TV channel, broker or wife) or he blames himself (guilty that he refused to attend a family dinner party that would have cost only ₹4000 and lost ₹40,000 in trades.) But he is still not ready to understand what exactly happened. On profit-making days, he doesn't feel the need to understand and on loss-making days, he is in no mood to understand. He is ready to stop trading the next day, but the following day, he gets good profits due to his lack of attachment. He buys two silver micros with fearless stoploss of just 500. Who fears a loss of ₹500 when they have lost ₹40,000? On that day, he gets 3500 in two micro lots. He is not happy. He repents. Why hadn't he gone for two big 30kg lots? But now he is back in the game.

He is smart enough to find free tips here and there. But he's unable to see that he has not added a single rupee to his capital this way. He has made a pattern of repeating his mistakes and not seeing them. So what should he do? Learn the right system by removing mistakes day by day. If you can make 2% out of a capital of ₹10,000 it works out to ₹200 daily. Continue this for 30 days. Then multiply the volume gradually and stick to it for 60 days. Take a break if you are too occupied. It is enough to see the facts.

Some more technical observations

Ride the STOCKS in trend.

Buy(uptrend)

The stock is in an uptrend and cuts and goes above the 50 day MA or 200 day MA. The MA is in an uptrend. The parabolic SAR Dot is below price. Preferably, there is a MACD crossover at the bottom. Preferably, the ADX goes up above 16. EXIT when the parabolic SAR Dot is above price. There is a MACD crossover at the top. Whichever comes first.

SELL (DOWNTREND)

The stock is in a downtrend and cuts and goes down below the 50-day MA or 200 DMA. The MA is in a downtrend The parabolic SAR Dot is above price. Preferably, there is a MACD crossover at the top. Preferably, the ADX is going up. EXIT when the parabolic SAR Dot is below price. There is a MACD crossover at the bottom. Whichever comes first.

STOCK BREAKOUT

(Breakout on the upside) The stock is trending sideways. There is a Bollinger squeeze. Place a buy stop above the resistance line and a sell stop below the support line. EXIT when the parabolic SAR Dot is above price. There is a MACD crossover at the top.

(Breakout negative)

The stock is trending sideways. There is a Bollinger squeeze. Place a buy stop above the resistance line and sell stop below the support line. EXIT when the parabolic SAR Dot is below price. There is a MACD crossover at the bottom.

HOW to see the mcx/stock market technical chart and what to see?

What to see in charts regularly?

1. **Trading range** in a day, month and year means how many points difference is there between the highs and lows of that period?

2. Try to find **some repeating patterns**?

    How long does it take to repeat?

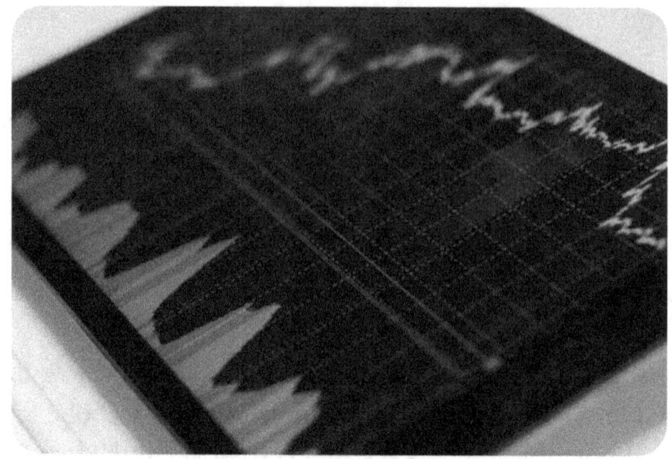

3. See details of the **behaviour of movements**. Does it move periodically or are there sudden, sharp moves?

4. Does it go downside to touch support before jumping ahead? **(FROG LEAP move)**

5. What is the **corelation** between this scrip and the sectoral index and the corelation between broad market index like NIFTY/ SENSEX/CNX midcap50 or COMDEX.

6. Do you find some **narrow and broad ranges** of price? The broad range comes after how many narrow ranges?

7. How can you use these ranges practically? Record daily prices and identify **fool proof methods** for cash or futures or options hedging.

8. See the corelation of two or three more scrips from the same sectors?

9. **Ups and downs of volume** with up and down prices and see gaps of increasing/decreasing volume.

10. See particular **timing patterns** in intraday and quarterly moves.

YOU ARE RIGHT BUT EARLY OR LATE

If you expect a reversal today, it doesn't happen tomorrow. It is gap down again and you've lost all your hope and the market reverses suddenly from there. When there is no hope for a reversal after a continuous fall, it will be a definite reversal. So go ahead with the double stop loss strategy or hedging with calls and puts. Nifty was supposed to reverse at 8500. It fell to 8400, 8300, and 8200 and it was a hopeless situation. If you bought at 8500, single side without hedging, it's a mistake. If you think of selling single sided at 8100 Nifty Futures level, it is the same mistake repeated.

So what you expect is not wrong; if you expect it in the next three days, it will happen after 13 days. There are TRIPPLE TOP patterns during picks of any scrip, and TRIPPLE BOTTOM patterns during bottoms of any scrips. That's why bottom fishing becomes so difficult to execute.

When a trader waits for some stock price to go in one direction desperately, and it goes up and down in cycles, it creates a loop of hope and fear which shatters his conviction. It is similar to rocks that suffer cracks due to the dramatic and frequent changes in weather. I call this WEATHERING and it happens due to frequent price fluctuations. Traders or investors should maintain an optimum distance to avoid weathering.

FUNDAMENTAL ANALYSIS

Fundamental analysis tells us what and why to buy, so it is considered a basis of good investment. But most traders ignore fundamental analysis, because they think it is useful for investors only. I insist you trade in fundamental stocks, because these stocks are favourite picks of MF and FII. You will not only enjoy huge profit margins, but you will also distance yourself from huge disasters due to the quality of the stocks. I will simplify this complex topic. The most important terms of fundamental analysis are given below:

EPS – Earnings Per Share

EPS means actual net profit of any business. It has nothing to do with the stock price appreciation. Market prices follow good EPS.

EPS = net profit / total number of shares issued.

Search for the TOP 100 EPS stocks on google. You can find a list of 100 stocks by clicking money control links suggested by google.

Equity capital = face value * total number of shares

Paid up capital = Issue price * total number of shares

Market capital = CMP * total number of shares

Market capital defines the size of a company, whether it is large cap, mid cap or small cap business. Huge market capital ensures SAFETY of invested funds, but EPS denotes profitability which is the main factor for better RETURNS.

SHARE HOLDING

Share holding patterns show the holdings of various types of market participants in a particular company.

Promoter holding: If this is good, the stock price will be more stable. If promoter increases his holdings through BUYBACK, it shows more reliability. If the promoter sells his stake, then the market reaction to such news might be very bad.

FII holding: Foreign institutional investors are major participants causing big rallies or downfalls. The FII holding shows high volatility in stocks.

MF holding: Mutual funds holding is most dependable. They are not allowed to trade very short term by SEBI. So, MF will never ignore the fundamental strength of their stock picks. Search for the top 100 MF holdings on Google.

TRENDLYNE is also a very good website that shows the quarterly changes in the holdings of MF, FII and promoters.

BOOK VALUE

BOOK VALUE shows the actual assets of a company.

(Paid capital + reserves) / total number of ordinary shares = book value

Price to book value ratio shows that the stock price is undervalued or inflated.

Google search P/BV ratio of stock. You will find many free websites like screener that shows these results.

Balance sheet of ABC Ltd

Market price per equity share – Rs 22

Ratio for SE limited:

EPS = Net profit – tax / number of ordinary shares outstanding = 33cr / 10cr = Rs 3.30 per share

Dividend yield = Dividend per share / market value per share * 100 = 2 / 22 * 100 = 11%

Price to earnings ratio = Market price of share/EPS = 22 / 3.30 = ₹6.66

Return on Equity = Net income after tax / Equity = 3.30 / (10.00+15.20)*100 = 13.09%

Debt to equity ratio = debt / Equity

= (14.30 + 16.90) / (10.00 + 15.20) = 1.24

Current ratio = Current assets / current liabilities

= 23.40 / 10.50 = 2.29

Quick ratio = Quick assets / current liabilities

= (0.20 + 11.80) / 10.50 = 12.00 / 10.50 = 1.14

Inventory turnover ratio = Cost of goods sold / inventory

= 55.20 / 10.60 = 5.20

Average collection period = receivables / average sales per day

= 11.80 / 70.1*1/360 = 61 days

Fixed assets turnover ratio = net sales / fixed assets

= 70.10 / 34.00 = 2.06

Gross profit ratio = gross profit / net sales

= 14.90 / 70.10*100 = 21%

Net profit ratio = net profit / net sales

Fundamental analysis tool kit

Picking quality stocks is the most important task for traders or investors.

KEY fundamental terms to check in good companies to compare and choose:

EPS

Book value (P/BV) ratio

ROCE

Below are FREE of cost tools on websites for continuous study and practicing swing trading with low volumes.

In.investing.com

Fundamental section

Screener.in (Four most powerful screens)

Safal niveshak

Bluest of blue chips

Darwas scan

Warren buffet screener

Coffee can portfolio

Top 100 EPS stocks

Sector wise details (peer group) moneycontrol

Trendlyne

Broker report

Mf /fii holding

Pittroski score

Check any stock for these three scores (DVM) on trendline:

Momentum score

Valuation score

Durability score

More than enough?

Wealth creation is a spiritual process.

I achieved financial freedom at the age of 40 only. I kept observing all my seniors, colleagues and juniors to confirm traditionally prevailing assumptions of the future and my security. My father had limited resources. He was in a very good government officer's post and accumulated a little for his children's future. But he always felt he had **more than enough**. And now I see that it has become a solid reality. He invested in love, shared knowledge and time with family which gave real returns. See my video with my father published April 21, 2020, on my YouTube channel. I too ran behind money for a few years, but I felt there was a big misconception. I thought that I would be more loved by my family after financial success because all my near and dear ones talked about career and money all the time. But my success created a new distance between me and them. Maybe it was because of lack of time or perhaps I had lost the patience I had had during my early struggles. I had lost my well-earned money once in the middle of my career. I had to spend two to three years without work, money and illusionary social satisfaction. It was scary in the beginning but it felt normal after a period. You don't feel the cold after the first minute under a cold shower.

Saari thand ek lota pani tak he.

When no one gives a fuck about you, then you have time to do things which you should have prioritised. I went to a few meditation camps. I read new things and worked on my health too. I felt that it should have been my first priority but traditional assumptions keep you running all the time whether you feel okay about it or not.

I kept noticing my wealthy friends but their problems increased with accumulation. So it was essential to learn when and where to stop. This is a very personal question. The answer depends on your background. Money alone provides very little motivation. There are always some emotional urges hidden behind every big success story.

The more than enough feeling gave me a real boost. I could go to Mumbai and then Goa with emotional reasons. I couldn't sustain the struggles of change. I tried to become professional at every milestone but that troubled my natural growth every time. Then I learned to go with the flow and felt it was more than enough. It required much patience to reach the right answers and those answers were capable of creating magic.

LONG TERM INVESTMENT CROREPATI PLAN FOR EVERY INDIAN

If one makes long-term investments, it minimises the risks. Profits in the long run are greater than short-term and day-trading profits. Holding a stock for more than a year is considered long-term officially, but more than three to five years is actually considered long-term. Many traders bought HUL at 200, sold it at 400 in two years, but those who did not sell have benefited more since the stock price is ₹2300. They can reap the same profits by selling just half their holdings. Some long-sighted fathers leave the deliveries of shares for their children. Such portfolios are worth crores of rupees. There are many ups and downs in the long-term. One has to keep a close watch and let it all happen. Stocks with good fundamentals should be chosen for long-term investments. Get ready with study accumulate savings in dips. There is a financial cycle in almost all asset classes which keeps repeating at particular intervals. There have been picks in the market after every four years. For example in 1992, 1996, 2000, 2004, 2008, 2012, and 2016. The pick may sustain for one or two years and the market keeps falling for the next three years. It is quite demotivating to hear that the market remains more in the bottom than ups. But this is very good news for a regular investor because he can keep buying 75% quantity at 25% cost and the money will multiply four times in four years. Two basic rules should be followed:

- The first is **diversification**. Invest in all major sectors because there will be sector shifts.

- The second is **cost averaging**. There is no right price for bad stocks and no wrong price for good stocks.

What is sector shift?

Sectors which run in the last bullish phase of the market (say 2006, 2007, 2008) fall dramatically from their picks, but all traders who entered the market in the last bull run are infatuated with these sectors and stocks, so they keep accumulating and get trapped in sectors like realty, metal, sugar, cement and infrastructure. Some sectors and stocks are out of the scene. Traders don't watching them at all (pharma stocks, auto, FMCG, Engineering etc). In this bull run, they suddenly pick up and become three to four times their value and will keep increasing till they reach the pick of this bull phase. New traders will get trapped in these sectors and stocks too. Many so-called investors recall that there was a time when Infosys, Reliance and LT were issued at ₹10 only. What if they had bought the stocks then? Sorry, bro, it was very difficult to buy those stocks at ₹10 then. If it was possible then it is still possible today. So many new Infosys, Reliance and LTs are in the making and you may miss this opportunity again with the same old attitude. There is very good news for you. You will always have a chance to buy a great stock at minimum price. As it was there on 21000 Sensex level in 2008, infy was less than half. It was the same story with HUL and Grasim. There is no mistake possible in the long-term because your money has zero value in your hands. All other investments are safer than you and your family's urge to continuously spend. There's no patience required for long-term investments because everyone has more than enough. If you can invest in money back insurance with all binding conditions for 25 years to earn a return that is only three to four times the investment and it covers a negligible risk, then cut down your patience to one third. A fixed deposit will double in 12 years. So any stock on Nifty or the Sensex can be bought with freedom of tenure and amount. Even gold and real estate will test your patience more than equity.

Historical studies will give you all the answers pertaining to the stock market ups and downs. This SIP calculator online shows detailed records of regular investments and their substantial gains.

System to invest in the long-term

Keep a record of your daily expenses. Restructure and analyse expenses and see what can be saved? A minimum of 10 to15% can be saved easily without giving up too much. For example, you spend ₹30,000 a month, so ₹3000 to ₹4000 is the wastage. Annually, it works out to ₹40,000. Whether your income goes up or not, your expenses certainly will. So, it may be like ₹1.2 lac in the first three years, then ₹1.8 lac in the next three years and so on. So 1.2 + 1.8 + 2.7 + 4 + 6 + 9 + 14 + 20 + 30 + 40 + 50 lacs = ₹1.9 crore. This will be the basic investment on your side. Because you will have a chance to book profits in the first five years, you can enter the market again in dips, buying double or triple the quantity from profits only. This is the most challenging period. If your portfolio remains alive for this period, then you will remain here for the next 30 to 50 years or as long as you are alive. After that, you will not be here, but the portfolio will still be with your loved ones.

Hurdles in long-term investment.

1. I don't have spare money. That is the general excuse. Investments should not be made from income. It should be made from expenses. So, even a student or housewife who spends ₹7k to ₹8k as pocket money can save ₹700 to ₹800 in wastage. One student can have a ₹2 crore portfolio just by buying stocks worth ₹700 per month. He has more time to let it grow.

2. Don't know the right stocks to buy? Buy any stock from Nifty/ Nifty midcap or Sensex. You will get good returns from all other asset classes even if 20% of those companies go bankrupt.

HOW to choose the right stock to buy?

You should buy 60% large cap stocks, 20% midcap stocks and 20% small cap stocks. Large cap will protect your capital, midcap will give you more growth and small cap will give you the maximum yield. If you have ₹1000 per month, then see the monthly losers on Nifty/Nifty midcap. If you see realty at the bottom, then you can buy 50 Unitech or 5 dlf and some small cap stocks.

Keep a balance among the all-time high stocks and the 52-week-low fundamentally strong stocks.

The next month, if metals are down, then 10 Hindalco stocks may be bought. You should buy stocks with a low price at the bottom as well as stocks at pick at double or triple the price. Suppose you buy dlf at ₹200 and it goes down to ₹120. At the same time you buy Sun Pharma at 500 and Maruti at 3000. They were near high but still you bought it in a little dip. So your portfolio is well-diversified. If DLF is losing at 40%, then these two stocks compensate for this loss with +70%. You can book big part profits in gaining stocks here and it may be reinvested in little parts in losing stocks in every dip. If your portfolio valued at ₹1 lac goes down to ₹90,000, it's okay. People are mentally prepared to see a 10 to 15% fluctuation in the stock market. But if the value dips to ₹60,000, then no one can console you for such a loss. The value may still go down further. This is why investors flee from the market never to return. Don't choose stocks by seeing the price only. Cheap is not cheap here and expensive is not expensive in investment. In the next 12 months, you will have 15 to 20 stocks spread across all the major sectors. Don't cost average by price but use the right time interval. So, you need not guess low in any falling stock because it is wrong in 90% of the cases.

1/3 rule for accumulation

If you want to accumulate some stocks in bottom fishing, then you should use this fantastic rule. Suppose you buy Unitech. It was ₹500 at some point in time, then it came down to ₹200. The investor keeps accumulating in every dip. Then it goes down to ₹70, then ₹25 and finally ₹6. So, if you buy and plan to hold for five years, then the purchasing process should go on for 5/3 = 1.5 years. This means, if you buy at six month intervals three times, then you will have gotten all the best levels giving you the best cost averaging. The same rule may be applied for selling as well. You sell Maruti at ₹3000. After three months, it goes up to ₹3600 and three months later you sell it at ₹4600. One can't guess LOW or HIGH in such a market and no one should try to make a guess. Let it happen first, the actual lows and highs will be before your eyes.

When and how to book profits (sell stocks)

There are two right reasons to sell. First, you need the money. This is the reason why you do everything but ask yourself whether it is a necessity or a luxury? Actually, you forgo small luxuries to afford big luxuries in the long run. Do not sell more than is essential. Sell with very tight hands. There is a saying: The rich fellow always plans to buy assets and the poor fellows always plans to sell assets. Second, picks in markets. You should keep booking part profit in jumps of the index and you should follow the 1/2/3 rule to sell stocks. Sell 5% of the portfolio in the first jump, 10% in the second jump and 15% in the third jump. Then, the market may show some profit-booking. Buy some good stocks again in dips. Do not try to sell more in jumps and buy in dips for short term joy. If you want to enjoy the chicken then don't be tempted to eat the omelette.

Otherwise, you will laugh at others who hold. You will boast about your frequent buying and selling four times. Meanwhile, you continue to cry for years over selling your entire portfolio on the first jump only. The other traders may be dull four times, but when they start laughing, they will keep laughing for years. For example, you buy Reliance Infra in 2004-05 and have several chances to buy at ₹400-500 and sell at ₹600-700, but once it breaks the 52-week high at ₹750, it breaks the all-time high at ₹1100 and reaches ₹2700. The same has happened in the Sensex levels and several stocks when the Sensex doubled in two years, (7000 level). Investors thought to sell 80% of their portfolio because they couldn't imagine it reaching 10000. You should get at least one dip to re-enter the market. The Sensex and Nifty did not give traders any chance to enter the market again. This happened with the traders who held for many months and sold on early jumps, waiting for a particular price to re-enter the market with good quality stocks. But they missed the rally eventually.

Study mutual funds for quality stocks. Don't touch stocks without good fundamentals. All of us are aware of the large cap or blue chip stocks, but midcap and small cap stocks are very difficult to recognize. So get the help of the top holdings of mid and small cap funds. I discuss many methods during telephonic training for very busy people in an easy manner. But it needs two-way communication due to the complex nature of the information.

Middle class traders are afraid to lose their hard-earned capital.

But there is one hidden thief which is stealing all their capital. It is INFLATION. If you can't beat inflation then you have lost already. People buy cars, TVs, and fridges and their value depreciates by half within two years. They will never go up. Their value will keep reducing to zero. But we are OK with this, so why should we worry about buying stocks which are down for the time being, but will go up again someday. You should look at your portfolio from a different angle. What is the value of your biggest dream? Just accumulating money may not be your biggest dream, but it can take you closer to your dream. One dreams of making crores of rupees over the next 30 years for the cost of one cold drink and a cigarette. (₹50/day means 1500/month.) I think dreams alone are enough to live life with great hope. Achieving your dream is secondary. What could be the worst case scenario here? Suppose you invested ₹10 lac over these 30 years. The market didn't support your investment which dips to ₹4 lac in value by the end of the period. This is almost impossible but just imagine it. You still profit by ₹4 lacs. HOW? Because if you hadn't started this process with a negligible amount, big hopes and total freedom to enter or exit, to stop or continue, there would have been a big zero. Because investment in any asset class is better than spending. Anticipating huge appreciation, traders invest in the stock market. A little appreciation in safe investments like FDs, RDs and insurance doesn't motivate youngsters. Our income is like the rains. It comes and goes. It is useful only when the earth absorbs the water. It is 10 to 15% only. In the same way, we earn and spend 90% of what we earn. We can save a maximum of 20%. This 20% is like a seed which may seem small but can yield huge returns. It is not enough to just to save more, but we must also sow it into the right soil. Asset classes have shown these results in last the 30 years.

FD average 9%

Gold 10.2%

Real estate average returns 14%

Equity 18%

So equity is the right asset class which can handle the inflation rate.

#Investment portfolio

If anyone has 2 lacs capital.

1 lac in secondary market 50 in liquid + 30 large + 20 small cap

1 lac in MF.

Or

1 lac in new IPO listing Switch in dips with 25% in four parts.

Fall with mutual funds And rise with equity.

What about #intraday? Holdings can be used as collateral for intraday trading.

Futures and options? If you are trading in futures and options, then leave everything. Invest ₹1 lac in trades and have ₹1 lac extra.

Only long-term and mutual funds should go parallel with a negligible amount like ₹5K to ₹10k per month. Whenever you want to leave the stock market in frustration due to failure, then stop trading but never stop investing, although it may be very small.

Back-office coordination

A broker invests in exchange membership by investing ₹1 to ₹3 crores. He distributes all his risk among sub brokers by taking ₹1 to ₹2 lacs in deposits from them. The sub broker takes the deposit cheques from clients to provide margins accordingly. If the client takes care of his own funds, then the sub broker is safe. If sub brokers are safe then the broker (member) is safe automatically. This is a fool proof system with proper risk distribution. There are many departments in a broker's head office. It is good to understand their workings and coordination for a sub broker.

1. **Account Opening – (CRC)**

   Client registration form (CRF) is submitted here with all relevant documents. Forms may be printed or in digital format now a days. Have a good relationship with this department for speedy processing of new accounts. If anything is missing, they will inform you at the earliest from their end.

2. **Survillence**

   This is a very important department. It manages the turnover limit for each client. It takes care of risk management for all sub brokers, which is the most important task here to survive.

3. **Accounts (pay in / pay out)**

   When the client has debit, then he has to submit a cheque here for PAY IN. If he has credit and wants to encash, he can request a PAY OUT here. Sometimes, the client gives the cheque but the accounts department doesn't credit it at that moment so the client may miss some big opportunity due to a five-minute delay in procedure.

4. **Depository operations**

   Depository deals with NSDL/CDSL. All demat processes are done here. This is useful for IPO (primary market) as well. Many investors hold very old share certificates which they are yet to dematerialize. They are not familiar with the new procedures and are busy with their own lives. If any sub broker lends a helping hand, he may get a potential client, because those 100 share certificates might turn into 1500 shares due to bonus issues. So this client may be worth ₹20 lacs now and he can give you a ₹2 lac cheque for trading at least.

5. **Networking and technology department**

The Networking Department handles lease line and ODIN/neat software issues. Mobile trading is also going to become popular. They can help your client to trade using their online account on their laptops and smart phones. If you keep talking to them frequently in a friendly manner, you will learn many technical things which will make you more efficient.

6. **Research and advisory**

Every broker has a special department for in-house technical and fundamental analysis. You may find some very good fellows to interact with. Sub brokers and clients keep watching and trading on their trading calls but they never try to interact with them properly. Keep talking to them at a suitable time. Ask precise questions and learn the science behind their trading tips.

7. **Marketing**

The marketing department is the most important department in bad and good times. So, it is given the most weightage. They are responsible for revenue growth. Seminars, events and marketing efforts by a team are done here. You can watch them and learn for your marketing plan. This department can support you officially or unofficially according to the company's business policies.

8. **In-charge OR Coordinator**

There is one head or in-charge who coordinates the workings of all the departments. You should have good relations with him and the other staff. Sub brokers can gift them occasionally and invest in building a relationship. Whenever you reach any department to resolve any problem, consider their issues. Try to understand the minute details of how all the departments work. It is better to have a friendly conversation instead of waiting with frustration. If you think that it's not your job, then you will remain a sub broker only. If you try to learn everything in this way, you may become a branch manager or trading member (main BROKER) someday. A good sub broker will try to answer all the client's questions which may not be directly related to him, but it makes the client feel that he can get all solutions under one roof. He goes nowhere else and keeps bringing new clients to the broker, more than any marketing executive.

COMMODITY TRADING GUIDE

MCX TRADING: SYSTEMATIC DAILY PLAN

1. First of all, check the global market, especially the data timing and note it down.

2. Then see the charts of all nine scrips for 21 days and six months on www.earnometer.com or www.moneycontrol.com.

3. If some scrip is gap up or gap down, then place buy above high and sell below low (trading robot model). Otherwise, hedge in two scrips after 11:30 a.m., which is more than 0.5% up or down. The same commodity hedging is safer (buy leadm Sep + sell leadm Oct).

4. Book a small profit once before 2:30 p.m.

5. You can apply the trading robot model. Place 18 buy/sell orders in nine scrips at 11:30 a.m. and keep booking fast profits in activated trade. NG and Mentha oil may give regular profits before 5:00 p.m.

6. Place four charts of four moving scrips (more than 0.5%) on screen and keep watching.

7. See the confirmed resistance and support of all scrips and select the two best scrips. Buy/sell with small SL at 5:54 or 6:29 p.m. Leadm / zincm daily hedging with 0.3 points SL suggested at 6:54 p.m.

8. Get prepared for crude inventory on Wednesday and NG inventory on Thursday at 8:00 p.m.

9. Book all profits till 7:00 p.m. generally.

10. If there is more than a 1.5% move in any scrip (specially gold / silver) then you can wait in micro lots with small SL till 9:30 p.m.

11. AVOID BTST in commodity markets without any big reason.

HOW TO CHOOSE THE RIGHT COMMODITY ON ANY DAY?

It is essential to choose the right commodity for trading on any day. If you are trading in THE wrong commodity (crude today after three days of an upward trend) you will remain frustrated in waiting and other commodities will pour the money on others. Some fellows are bound to gold and silver only while others are bound to copper and nickel only. It is not good for regular intraday profit. If silver has shown good moves for two to three consecutive days, then it has to be range-bound and volatile the next day. So come out of a hangover of a party-like move on time. Without any prior assumption just observe the screen with focus. Here's a real example: On June 27, 2013, the market was very negative. But the NICKEL remained in plus till the evening. Choose any such scrip which is falling dramatically in a good falling market. That scrip will go up in the small reversals of the negative market. BUY this scrip. Any scrip which doesn't moving up in a good upside market, will fall sharply in a small down fall. GOLD behaved this way on that day. SELL

IT. CHECK if it is below average continuously. The sellers increase and the sector is negative. If nickel is plus, copper is minus, then there is confusion in this sector. You should check the above given parameters for all commodities, one by one. It hardly takes five minutes. Then choose the strongest **(above average, more buyers, sector is strong, last three-day move)** and the weakest to sell **(below average, more sellers, sector down, last three days)**. There should be no panic in buying and selling. If you tried to buy silvermini (5kg) at ₹40,100 and it went up suddenly to ₹40,300, then buy two silvermicro (2kg) at ₹40,300 and the remaining in dip, if you get a chance. Trade during the right time slots. Six to 7:00 p.m. is the best due to LME opening.

Three types of hedging

Hedge means to protect your capital. So, when there is confusion, place trades in both directions till you have clarity with definite stop losses. Generally, traders know about hedging but not enough. It is a must to know how and when to open hedging and how to close?

Three main types of hedging

1. **Intra commodity hedging**: Hedging within the same commodity. Buy silver in January and sell silver in December with 300 points SL. This is safe.

2. **Intra sector**: Hedging within the same sector but different commodities. For example, you buy goldm at ₹28,800, SL ₹28,650, sell silvermini at ₹56,000, SL ₹56,380, buy copper at ₹406, SL ₹404, sell nickel at ₹940, SL ₹948. RISK – 2000 IN BOTH LEADMINI and ZINCMINI WITH 1/ – SL. During the day, book small tgt on both sides. Big tgt is possible from 6:00 to10:00 p.m.

3. **INTER SECTOR**: Hedging in different sectors. This is more risky when it is clear that the market is red. Sell gold and nickel when the market is clearly green. Buy gold and nickel or buy silver and copper when in confusion. Buy strong bullion, sell weak base metals (according to the buyer/seller ratio). It becomes dangerous because sometimes you hit SL on both sides. When

Comdex is less than + 30 or – 30 points, the bullion goes up and base metals take a breather. When Comdex is more than + 50 or – 50 points, all commodities go bullish or bearish at the same time. THIS IS CALLED ALL ROUND BULLISHNESS / BEARISHNESS. In such a market, buy on each dip and sell on each jump at 5:55 p.m., 6:55 p.m., 7:55 p.m., 8:55 p.m. and 9:55 p.m. or sell on each jump in all commodities but with a strictly small SL and book small profits very fast.

HOW TO HANDLE HEDGING?

Hedging means protection of your capital. Many traders buy July silver and sell August silver with NO STOPLOSS. This is not hedging because even after a 5000 point movement, you will not get anything. When you close one side, you are completely exposed to risk on the other. So hedging should be with a maximum of 0.5% stoploss on both sides. If you take a 200 point SL in July buy and August sell, and Silver moves 1% in any direction, then you will get 500 points in one direction and – 200 points SL in the other direction. Net profit is + 300 points. It is not essential that you earn profit every time in hedging. Sometime, it moves 200 points on one side and reverses to hit SL on the other side. In this case, If you have hedging of 2 lots July buy and 2 lots August sell, stoploss hits on one side. Suppose buy side then at least buy 1 lot again with same sl. The rule is to keep open both sides till the desired profit.

OR

Close both sides when one side hits SL. What is the benefit in hitting an SL of 200 points on one side and getting 200 points on the other side? Brokerage fees + taxes are also extra losses? In fact, hedging gives you the desired profits only three times out of 10. So why must you use this tool? It gives you support till you reach clarity. Suppose crude swings above and below the average. You hedged and got 10 points and lost 10 points SL. If you had hit two SLs on a single side of 15 points, then your trading window shows a loss of 3000. After seeing such figures in red, a trader loses his balance and he suffers fresh losses. If you see your window with no profit, and no losses till the evening, when the clear move occurs, you will end up with some profit by the end of the day. Some people over-trade; hedging keeps them engaged with no losses. Good observation starts with no fear at all DURING HEDGING. You may not miss any big reversal, if you hedge regularly (morning and evening). There are some problems also. Hedging cuts your profit by half, but you can get it frequently with one fourth of the risk. Beginners are very confused with hedging due to emotional involvement. Don't worry and face the first 10 bad days for lifelong tension-free skills.

DETAILS OF MAIN COMMODITIES IN MCX

Gold

This is the most traded commodity scrip in mcx India. There are four different lot sizes. Gold petal – 1 gram. This is best for practice to place orders with speed. Any mistake done will cause minimal losses. Gold guinea – 8 grams. Goldmini –100 grams, Gold –1kg. Gold is defensive in comparison to silver in the bullion sector. Gold shows a clear direction in single side. Stop loss value: Min. 40p to 100p ₹400 to 1000 – in gold mini.

Hedging: It goes along with silver so hedging is suitable with silver. One goldm with 40 point stop loss + 3 silvermic with 150 point stop loss is a suitable hedging combination. Daily hedge with the same commodity Buy goldm in January + sell goldm in February at 11:54 a.m., 2:29 and 5:54 p.m. Stop loss 30p, tg 80p, single side daily trade. Keep the stop loss. Buy at high and sell at low with 30p to 70pt target. This is especially effective in the bottoms and picks of goldm.

IMPORTANT WEB SITES

www.gfms.co.uk | www.lbma.org.uk | www.nymex.com |

www.tocom.com.jp | www.gold.org |www.kitco.com |

www.dmcc.ae | www.iab.gov.tr | www.usagold.com

SILVER–

There are four different lot sizes. Silvermic –1kg MICRO. This is best for practice to place orders with speed. Any mistake done will cause minimal loss. Silverm – 5kg, Silver – 30kg. Silver is volatile in comparison to GOLD in the bullion sector. Silver can show a swing in both sides. Stop loss value: Min. 80p to 180p, ₹300 to ₹600 in three silver micros.

Hedging: It goes along with gold so hedging is suitable with Gold. One goldm with 40 point stop loss + three silvermic with 150 point stop loss is a suitable hedging combination. Daily hedge with the same commodity. Buy three silvermic in February + sell three silvermic in April at 11:54 a.m., 2:29 p.m. and 5:54 p.m. SL 100p, tg 250 – 600p. Single side daily trade. Keep stop loss buy at weekly high + sell at weekly low with 100 to 400 points target. This is especially effective in bottoms and picks with a flexible target. Check the upbreak out (weekly high) and down breakout (weekly low) on earnometer website commodity section.

COPPER

There are two different lot sizes. COPPER – 1MT (1 METRIC TON), Copper –250kgs. Copper is volatile in comparison to nickel in the base metal sector. Stop loss value: Min. 0.5 points to 1 point, ₹130 to ₹300 in copper mini.

Hedging: It goes along with nickel so hedging is suitable with nickel. One copperm with 1 point stop loss + three nickelm with 1 point stop loss is a suitable hedging combination. Daily hedge with the same commodity Buy one copperm in February + sell 1 copperm in April at 11:54 a.m., 2:29 p.m. and 5:54 p.m. SL 0.6p, tg 1.5 – 3points, single side daily trade. Keep the stop loss buy at weekly high + sell at weekly low with 1 to 4 points target. This is especially effective in bottoms and picks with a flexible target.

NICKEL

There are two different lot sizes.

NICKEL – 250kg, NickelM – 100kg.

Nickel is volatile compared to copper in the base metal sector. It may swing from red to blue and blue to red twice a day. Stop loss value: Min. 1.5 points to 3 points, ₹150 to ₹300 in nickel mini. Hedging: It goes along with copper so hedging is suitable with copper. One copperm with 1 point stop loss + three nickelm with 1 point stop loss is a suitable hedging combination. Daily hedge with the same commodity. Buy 1 nickelm in December + sell 1 nickelm in January at 11:54 a.m., 2:29 p.m., and 6:54

p.m. SL 2p, tg 5 – 12 points, single side daily trade. Keep stop loss buy at weekly high + sell at weekly low with three to seven points target. This is especially effective in bottoms and picks with a flexible target.

It may show a reversal of 15 to 25 points from bottom and pick. Average daily move (12 of 22 trading days) +1.5 to – 1.5%. Extreme move (3 to 4 out of 22 trading days) + 3% or 3 – 4% 5 to 6 days will show extreme volatility with both sides swing or a very tight range-bound dull day after any big move.

As societies develop, their demand for metal increases based on their current economic position, which is also referred to as the national economic growth factor.

www.lme.co.uk

www.basemetals.com

www.kitco.com

www.futuresource.com

www.insg.org | www.nidi.org | www.metalbulletin.com

|www.basemetals.com | www.barx.com

www.international.standardbank.com|

www.futuresource.com | www.metalsmarket.net |

www.metalsplace.com | www.metalprices.com |

www.brookhunt.com | www.gfms-metalsconsulting.com

WWW.reuters.com /finance/commodities

WWW.KITCO.COM

WWW.CRBtrader.COM

WWW.lme.com

LEAD

LEAD – 5MT and zinc show almost the same moves and behaviours in the base metal sector. They are not directly coupled with copper or nickel. It may show a tight range for hours, then a sudden move of 2 to 3%. Stop loss value: Min. 0.25pt (25paisa) to 0.4pt. ₹250 to ₹400 in lead mini. Hedging: It goes along with zinc so hedging is suitable with zinc. One leadm with 1 point stop loss + 1 zincm with 0.3pt stop loss is a suitable hedging combination. Even if there is a movement of 80 paisa, it will yield a profit of 0.8 – 0.3 = 0.5pt. Daily hedge with the same commodity. Buy one leadmini in December + sell one leadmini in January at 11:54 a.m. and 6:54 p.m. SL 0.3p, TARGET one to two points. Single side daily trade. Keep stop loss buy at weekly high + sell at weekly low with 0.7 to 2 point target. This is especially effective in bottoms and picks with a flexible target.

It may show a reversal of two to four points from bottom and pick. Average daily move (12 of 22 trading days) + 1.5 to – 1.5%. Extreme move (3 to 4 out of 22 trading days) + 3% or 3 to 4% 5 to 6 days will show extreme volatility with both sides swinging or a very tight range-bound dull day after any big move.

ZINC

There are two different lot sizes:

ZINC – 5MT, Zincmini – 1MT.

Lead and zinc show almost the same moves and behaviour in the base metal sector. They are not directly coupled with copper and nickel. It may show a tight range for hours and then a sudden move of 2 to 3%. Stop loss value: Min. 0.25pt (25paisa) to 0.4pt, ₹250 to ₹400 in zinc mini.

Hedging: It goes along with lead so hedging is suitable with lead. One leadm with 1 point stop loss + one zincm with 0.3point stop loss is a suitable hedging combination. Even if there is a movement of 80 paisa, it will yield a profit of 0.8 to 0.3 = 0.5 points. Daily hedge with the same commodity. Buy 1 zincmini in December + sell 1 zincmini in January at 11:54 a.m. and 6:54 p.m. SL 03p, tg1 to 2 points. Single side daily trade. Keep stop loss buy at weekly high + sell at weekly low with 0.7 to 2 point target. This is especially effective in bottoms and picks with a flexible target. It may show a reversal of two to four points from bottom and pick. Average daily move (12 of 22 trading days) + 1 to – 1%. Extreme move (3 to 4 out of 22 trading days) + 3% or – 3% 5 to 6 days will show extreme volatility with both sides swinging or a very tight range-bound dull day after any big move.

CRUDE

There is one lot size: CRUDE – 100 BBL.

Option trading is also becoming popular now a days, so you can earn huge profits with little capital and limited risk. Crude and Natural Gas (NG) are totally different and de coupled in the ENERGY sector. There is no corelation between these two like any other sector. Crude shows continuous movement in the afternoons and evenings. Stop loss value: Min. 6pt to 15 pt ₹60 to ₹150 in crude. You can buy or sell 1 to 2 lots. Hedging: Only same commodity hedging is possible. It can't be hedged with natural gas. Buy 1 crude oil in December and sell 1 crude oil in January. Stop loss 7 points, tg 20 to 60 points is a suitable hedging combination. Even if there is a movement of 17 points, it will yield a profit of 10 points. It will be 1000 in big lots.

Hedging with options-

Buy crude oil future in downfall + buy nearest OTM put.

Sell crude oil future on picks + buy near OTM call with good OI.

Traders with less capital but sound knowledge may trade in options to enjoy big rallies or free fall. Daily hedge with the same commodity. Buy crude M in December + sell crude M in January at 11:54 a.m., 2:29 p.m. and 6:54 pm sl6p tg12point, single side daily trade. Keep stop loss buy at weekly high + sell at weekly low with 9 to 22 points target. This is especially effective in bottoms and picks with a flexible target. It may show a reversal of 70 to120 points from bottom and pick. Average daily move (12 of 22 trading days) + 1 to – 1%. Extreme move (7 out of 22 trading days) + 3% or – 3%.

Four or five **inventory days** are there every Wednesday in a month. Inventory timing may be between 8:00 p.m. and 9:00 p.m. Open hedging just before one minute and book fast at dot time big move. The timing should be confirmed by the www.forexfactory.com website's economic calendar. Five to six days will show extreme volatility with both sides swinging after a continuous fall or rally forming double top/double bottom reversal.

NATURAL GAS – 125 BBL

NATURAL GAS – NG. No mini lot is available. Single lot size is there. WWW.reuters.com /finance/commodities. Crude and Natural Gas (NG) are totally different and de coupled in the ENERGY sector. There is no corelation between these two like any other sector. NG shows continuous movement in the afternoons and evenings. Stop loss value: Min. 0.40 points to 1 point, ₹500 to ₹1200 in 1 LOT. Buy defensive near ATP or resistance/support level, so that a small stoploss may work. It is good for day time movement. Hedging: same commodity hedging is only possible. It can't be hedged with crude. Buy 1 NG in December and sell 1 NG in January. SL 0.60 point, tgt 1 to 3 points is a suitable hedging combination. Even if there is a movement of 2 points, it will yield a profit of 1.4 points. It will be 1800 in a single lot. Daily hedge with the same commodity. Buy NG December + sell NG January at 2:29 p.m. SL 0.6p, tg 1 to 3 points, single side daily trade. Keep stop loss buy at weekly high + sell at weekly low with 1 to 3 points target. This is especially effective in bottoms and picks with a flexible target. It may show a reversal of 3 to 6 points from bottom and pick. Average daily move (12 of 22 trading days) +1 to – 1%. Extreme move (7 out of 22 trading days) +3% or – 3%. Four to five inventory days are there every Thursday of the month.

Inventory timing may be between 8:00 p.m. and 9:00 p.m. Open hedging just before one minute and book fast at dot time big move. Buy NG in December + sell NG in January at 7:59 p.m. SL 0.70 points, tgt 2 to 5 points. It may hit stop loss on both sides in inventory two out of five times a month. But you may get four to five points on two inventory days. So monthly gains may be 11-3 = 8 points. A single lot will give +10,000. Four lots may deliver +40,000 monthly. The timing should be confirmed on the www.forexfactory.com website economic calendar. There will be extreme volatility for five to six days with both sides swinging after a continuous fall or rally forming double top/double bottom reversal.

MENTHA OIL

No mini lot is available, only single lot size. MENTHA OIL is traded from 10:00 a.m. to 5:00 p.m. only. It shows daily movement during the day. Stop loss value: Min. 1.5 points to 3 points. ₹500 to ₹1100 in 1 LOT. Buy defensive near ATP or resistance/support level, so that a small stoploss may work. It is good for day time movement. Hedging: Same commodity hedging is only possible. Even if there is a movement of one point, it will yield a profit of 0.60 points. It will be 1000 in a single lot. Daily hedge with the same commodity. Buy mentha in December + sell mentha in January at 4:29 p.m. SL 1.5 points, 4 to 8 points, single side daily trade. Keep stop loss buy at high + sell at low with a 1 to 3 point target. This is especially effective in bottoms and picks with a flexible target. It may show a reversal of 12 to 30 points from bottom and pick. Average daily move: (12 of 22 trading days) + 2 to − 2%. Extreme move: (7 out of 22 trading days) + 4% or − 4%. So monthly gains may be 15%. A single lot will give + 20,000. Four lots may deliver + 80,000 monthly. The timing should be confirmed on the www.forexfactory.com website's economic calendar. There will be extreme volatility for five to six days with both sides swinging, after a continuous fall or rally forming a double top/double bottom reversal.

HOW TO READ THE ENTIRE MCX COMMODITY ONLINE SCREEN

(MARKET WATCH) IN FIVE MINUTES

Silverm crosses the ATP and goes beyond the − 0.5% range so buying has started. If buyers increase, then buying will confirm. Goldm behaves the same as silver. When CRUDE crosses the ATP, there will be more buyers, and more than 0.5% buying is there. Keep stop loss buying of nikelm above 445, SL 441, tgt 455, and stop loss selling below 439 and tgt 430. This is the cage technique designed by me. Trade will be activated after clarity only. Zinc is stronger than leadm. They try to come up. Hedging (zincm buy/leadm sell SL 0.3 both sides, tgt 1 to 2 points. Buy Ng medium but reversal between 2:00 and 5:00 p.m. is possible. It is already on pick. Be cautious. It may be range bound the whole day, but a sharp move may happen any time after 3:00 p.m. I shall send you the calls, but if a sudden move happens you can try my trading rules with silvermic and nikelm, SL 150 points and 3 points. Sometimes, the market doesn't give the advisor a chance to type and send the message. Trading on your own gives you real confidence. But don't overtrade. If you lose 500 to 1000, then don't do further trades on that day.

HOW TO ADD PROFITS IN A RALLY?

Multiple lots with minimum risk trading is like fishing. You just keep sitting with your tools and waiting. The fish may arrive within two minutes or you may have to wait for hours. NO one knows when it will happen. On July 26, 2013, Comdex was totally red. Gold was red with a minimum minus percentage indicating that it was relatively strong. In the downside market, all commodities may be red. You need to identify the commodities near ATP, as they tend to come up in each recovery. This will be the best commodity to buy. That is why I chose the GOLDM buying call. Goldm was running at ₹26,375 at that time. If the entire market goes down further and there is no recovery at all, then buying in any commodity will be risky. So, I adopted caution. I gave a stoploss, buying above the day's resistance at ₹26,450. The stoploss was 50 points (₹26,400). When buying is activated above ₹26,450, and becomes stable above that level, you can buy three more lots in a small dip near ₹26,420 and ₹26,430. SL is ₹26,400. Extra risk will be – 600 for three lots. In a sudden recovery, goldm went to ₹26,570. You can buy three lots with almost 70 to 120 points and get +3000 in – 1000 SL. When you multiply lots, then book part profits fast in any positive wave, or book part losses in a negative wave. It's not good to hit the SL of 5 lots in a single shot. You can exit in 3 lots and may re-enter at lower levels.

21 AUGUST MCX TRADING LESSON

(The dollar hit an all-time high and there was a sudden up move in bullion)

ON August 21, 2013, silver and gold were weak in the morning. They touched the support level at – 0.5%. Then, they bounced back from there at 2:00 p.m., when the dollar hit an all-time high. This supported all commodity markets, especially bullion (gold and silver). On the morning of August 22, I watched a sudden move in one direction. So, I gave a sell call at noon in nickel and silver with a small stop loss (2pt/150pt). This call was very successful. Due to the upward move of the dollar on August 21, the stock market suddenly crashed from + 250 points to – 250 points, especially the banking sector. I gave a NG call in the morning. It was range bound from 217 to 217.6. I opted for defensive buying at 217 lower end and set SL at 216.4 (the very next support level as shown in the chart). It went without any break to 225. You can book profits frequently and re-enter at every small dip with 0.3 SL or you can trail the stoploss at the next level. That target was achieved at 2:00 p.m. NG remained rangebound for the next five to six hours (223-225).

After a big profit, you should focus on other commodities. I picked a silvermicro sell call with 150pt SL. That SL hit in a sharp upward move. You can't send so many calls in one message. It may be risky for a slow or small trader. So buy on crossover (minus to plus or below to above ATP crossover). Use our small stoploss methods in such a fast movement only once or twice (300-500) and book profits fast. It will give you self-confidence. Several traders practice my techniques instead of any advisory's trading calls and have doubled and even tripled their profits. In the evening, when silver was in the ₹51,450 to ₹51,550 range, it gave a clear signal that silver would hit the 51200-50800 support level first, then it would go up again. If silver is + 2 to 2.5% before 3:00 p.m. and becomes rangebound, then between 3:00 p.m. to 6:00 p.m., there's a 70% chance that it will come near ATP or the day's most touched support level. You may call us and we will show you that support in your own Odin chart over the phone. The last call in silver was to buy only above the day's high of ₹51,400. The high broke after 8:30 p.m. and it made a new high twice (51680-51780) within 10 minutes. (0.5% more than the previous high) Always think in terms of percentage, not in terms of points only.

GOLDM hedging on July 17 (the bull riding story)

There had been a tight range since the last eight trading days. Many small stop losses hit. The numerous stop losses leave traders in despair, even though the amount is negligible. On this day, I finally decided to focus on a single commodity with hedging. First of all, I bought goldm on August 2 at ₹26,600 SL ₹26,565 (35 points sold on September 2 when goldm stood at ₹26,590, SL ₹26,620 (stoploss 30 points, it was a 700 risk on any side. Goldm jumped 30 points up and hit the SL at 11:05 a.m. It was the time to book profits on August 1. BUY and sell again on September 1 with a 30 point SL. This means to sell at ₹26,630, SL 26,660. But this movement was very fast. Slow traders and those trading over the phone reacted when goldm bought in August came down to ₹26,580 near buying SL of ₹26,565. I advised to sell goldm bought in September with a 40 point SL. Then, GOLDM came down to ₹26,550. This low was touched two to three times from 12:15 p.m. to 1:55 p.m. It hit the SL of ₹26,565 with the August buy. Till this time, loss in 1 lot buy and 350 gains in 1 lot sell + 300. If you did not book profits in 1 buy lot then SL 700 gains + 350 = – 350. I decided to keep position on both sides till evening. So I bought August GOLDM again at ₹26,560, SL 26,520. Finally, it jumped at 6:00 p.m. to ₹26,680, (+130 points). Now it was clearly more than 0.5%. The buyers had doubled. The second jump came between 5:55 p.m. and 6:05 p.m. It went to ₹26,840 (+290 points) and came to ₹26,680 after just ten minutes at 6:15 p.m. It touched ₹26,770 again after an hour and a half at 7:45 pm (+ 90 points). At 8:15 p.m., there was a big reversal. Goldm suddenly came down to ₹26,400. (NOTICE THAT FROM 7:55 p.m. TO 8:30 p.m., the MARKET TOOK A BREATHER OR WITNESSED A REVERSAL). After booking a big profit, if you expect further profits from there, then open position with hedging only. The FINAL GAIN POSSIBLE WAS 3000 +1500 = 4500 IN 2 CHANCES of goldm only. NICKELM, LEADM, NG also witnessed a clear move in the evening. They REVERSED from 7:55 p.m. to 8:15 p.m. I had said in an earlier article that Mondays and Tuesdays are dull rangebound days and Wednesdays and Thursdays show clear big moves (crude, Ng inventory respectively). Fridays are okay.

HOW SHOULD WE DEAL WITH CRUDE/NATURAL GAS INVENTORY DATA?

The average is generally the weighted average of high and low of that period. The period may be a day, week or a year. If some commodity or scrip remains above ATP, then it is said to be strong on the buy side. If it slips to below average, then it becomes weak (sell). For example, CRUDE was near the average of ₹5720. After some struggles, it came up fairly above ₹5720 with increasing buyers. In this situation, two options are possible for trading. First, buy crude at ₹5728 SL 5719 or buy crude June and sell crude July, stoploss 8 points on both sides. Hedging will give you support till you gain clarity. Generally, a 40 to 50 point stoploss in crude is given by tippers all over India. If you hit 16 points SL on both sides on a very bad day, then you will get three fair chances at the same 50 point risk. It's not possible to hit three stop losses consecutively, if you enter at 6:15, 7:15 and 8:15 p.m. Now crude goes up to ₹5790. The average is still at ₹5732. It is 50 to 60 points above the average. Generally, this scrip slips to the average once, then bounces back again (only if the data supports it). So what should you do here at ₹5790? Book once buying profit, then sell at ₹5790, SL 5800 or buy June crude and sell July crude again with 8 points SL on both sides. This ATP phenomenon may be seen in other scrips too.

Crossover

If you want to earn huge profits in minutes just process on crossover. Keep the charts of three to four commodity scrips open. See the most common line on the chart that is touched many times buy price line. In the case of the stock market, keep watching the sector every two hours and check Nifty, Nifty junior or Nifty midcap list as well to identify any sector or stock that shows a sudden upward trend. Buy it with minimum possible SL 2 paisa say 0.25% dimate. Book profit within 10 or 30 minutes and exit after every big move to book profits.

Types of crossovers

1. **If anything changes from red to green or green to red.**

2. **Above or below ATP.**

3. **Breaking strong resistance or support.**

4. **Breaking high or low.**

CRUDE OIL TRADE: Crude looks a very sharp deep last month. It is again trying to break it's all time low. There was a tight range yesterday morning. The low was ₹2865 and the high was ₹2878. So I kept stoploss buy above high of ₹2880 and stoploss sell below ₹2860. The range broke at 13:23 p.m. and made a low at ₹2861. Then, there was a sharp reverse. It hit a high at ₹2911 at 13:44 p.m.

TRADING ROBOT MODEL FOR MCX

The robot model for trading involves keeping a stoploss buying and selling in nine popular MCX commodities. Because when you expect movement in one commodity, then another commodity may have sudden movement, so you miss the opportunity. It was the same case today. There was a big change in the base metal and energy sectors. But the bullion was very dull in the morning. Suddenly, the bullion showed sudden movements. Goldm showed a positive breakout at 1:30 p.m. and moved up by 300 points. Such big moves always happen when very few traders expect it. Such big moves will not be repeated in the forthcoming days. HOW to create the MCX Commodity market watch?

1. List this series and the next series for all lots of nine main commodities.

2. Keep a gap between lines and use big font size due to fewer scrips.

3. Choose scrips more than 0.5%. Place them on the upper half and the lower half may be used for two charts in the lower two quarters if you have a single screen.

4. It is better to have a separate screen for charts. Four charts in four quarters. Maximize any chart to full screen if it breaks some support/resistance to see more detailed levels. How to trade defensive near chart and book smart profits? Buy defensive near support level after seeing the chart. Keep booking part profits while price goes upside with trailing stop loss. But do not trail stoploss after the second wave. Then, sell at jump and keep stoploss buy at high.

Abhimanyu complex

You might have heard the story of Abhimanyu in the Mahabharata. He learnt to enter the chakravyuha but did not know how to exit it. So he had to die. Everyone knows to enter the stock market but few know how to exit it. Forget what you have bought. Just see where it can take you. If you sold at a small loss and the stock goes up again subsequently, it is very painful. But this small loss can be recovered easily in a new rally. If you wait for recovery and the loss grows from 1000 to 3000 in the last three hours, then it is highly demotivating. You may start blaming yourself for hours. So don't wait any longer. Suppose you entered Nifty at ₹8500 call at 90. It reduced to 60 on the same day due to an unexpected sudden reversal. It caused a loss of 30*50 = 1500. Nifty breaks a big support in the charts, so there is no hope for easy recovery. But the loss seemed big that day, so you couldn't exit and had to bear a total premium loss on expiry. Stoploss is painful, but less than LOSS.

Cut your finger to save your hand.

THE 12 MOST POWERFUL TRADING STRATEGIES FOR 12 MONTHS ALL ROUND PRACTICE

(Full Proof TRADING MASTERY PLAN)

3:25 BTST (BUY TODAY SELL TOMORROW) STRATEGY

Be there at your screen at 3:10 p.m. Auto square off is done by all discount brokers. Now deliverable stocks might go up.

Go to the various **6 screeners** now. See the maximum volume and list these stocks to market watch.

15 minutes breakout

Bullish for the next day***

Intraday buying seen in the last 15 minutes

Short term breakout***

Volume shocker

Potential breaks out

It should take hardly10 minutes. At 3:25 p.m. check which stock from this market watch is still near the day's high. See the five-day chart and avoid it if it has already gained continuously for five days. Prefer if it picks up after correction. Choose midcap with low capital, but BTST won't be allowed in some stocks. Large cap can be taken with big volumes, large cap are allowed in intraday trade as well so you can short 50% intraday.

Book at 9:17 p.m. 70% quantity. Your target is to get 1% daily with free capital. Some mid and small caps are not allowed intraday, so don't put more than 30% of total capital in this. Less capital with big profit margin should be the formula in mid and small cap. Go with the new stock broker account that supports BTST.

All in one screener

Anyone can BUY this screener from the ZEROLOSS OPTION TRADE android app in the Google store. Click the link for the screener. Your main strategy should be fewer trades, more gains. These are the best stocks from all the best screeners. Click on the month high, day high and year high. Choose the minimum percentage difference from the highs. For intraday, trade at 9:40 and 10:30 am. Set the stoploss at 1% and leave the screen for 40 minutes. Return to it at 3:10 p.m. Watch the same screener. Put the top five stocks on market watch. If you have more than ₹2 lacs, then list stock futures with OTM puts. If you have anywhere between ₹20k to ₹80k, then equity cash is okay. You need 1 to 2% profit. This means, ₹200 to ₹400 from ₹20k. If it opens gap down, set SL at 1% from there. If it opens gap up, then book 70% and set stoploss at 1% with the remaining equity.

Study the previous night weekly breakout on this link. See the volume and chart. See short-term breakout the previous night. This is just to warm up for the next day. Watch the sector at 9:20 a.m. Buy/ sell nothing. Don't panic. Watch comfortably. You can't catch all and it's not needed too. At 9:25 p.m., check out on the given link, the intraday weekly breakouts. Check the highest volume. Buy 50-50 shares at cmp and 1% lower. If it's LTP near high, buy at high a bigger volume. Set stop loss at 60% of the volume. Buy small volumes if Nifty/stock has gone up in the last two days. Buy a bigger volume if the stock goes down drastically over the last two days. See weekly breakout for shorts. Leave the screen at 9:40 a.m.

Return to the screen at 1:20 p.m. See the sectors again. Buy stocks from the strongest sector. Buy a small quantity of short-term breakout after 3:10 p.m. Set stoploss at 1%. Keep it if there is an upper circuit. Let the profits stretch. If the morning is negative, don't panic. It will recover 80% times over. If you get ₹5000 from this strategy, then you can get premium paid services for ₹780 per month. Set an alert for one to two minutes. You will get SMSs and mails every hour.

All in one 3:25 p.m. strategy

Your main strategy should be to do fewer trades with more gains. These are the best stocks from all the best screeners. Click on the month's high, day's high and year high. Choose minimum percentage difference from the highs. For intraday, trade at 9:50 a.m. keep stoploss of 1% and leave the screen for 40 minutes. Return to the screen at 1:40 p.m. Watch the same screener. Put the top five stocks on market watch. If you have more than ₹2 lacs, then list the stock future with OTM put. If you have anywhere between ₹20k and ₹80k, then equity cash is okay. You need 1 to 2% profit. This means 200 to 400 from 20k. If it opens gap down, keep 1% SL from there. If it opens gap up, then book 70% and keep stoploss of 1% with the remaining.

Stock futures and options reversal strategy

If you want to be a successful trader, then study the day's tradings for 30 minutes at night and trade the following day for just 15 minutes. Check out the monthly gainers and losers, then weekly gainers and losers. Finally, check the trades over the last three days. Observe the global market at 9:00 a.m. Open the volume shocker page. You should have a market watch ready the previous night .

Check the open lows first to see if Nifty is positive. Check the LTP high. Buy one stock that took a dip in the last three days. Check open highs if Nifty / Sensex is negative and check the LTP low. Sell one stock which moved upside over the last three days.

Create a market watch for Nifty / bank Nifty futures with the 5-5 most active out of the money call puts listed there. Watch open low or open high condition here.

If Open-low same is strong BUY if LTP is still near day's high. **If Open-high same** is short SELL if LTP is still within 1% of day's low. Check out Nifty technical at earnometer.com and In.investing.com (15 minutes timeframe for intraday, 1 hour timeframe for positional).

Check the most active stock futures. Observe the earnometer futures screener. Create a market watch for bullish/bearish stocks with OTM call puts or stock options if you trade in these instruments. Don't focus on all the instruments simultaneously. Open From 9:20 to 9:30 a.m. Close till last at 11:00 a.m. Then, check index – sectoral indices at nseindia. com. Check percentage changes directly. Check the strongest or weakest sector. And place orders worth ₹20k defensive buy /defensive sell with 0.5% SL cover order.

Keep the following websites open: Nseindia, Nifty 50, Nseindia index, Volume shocker, Recovery from intraday low/ Fall from intraday high.

Place a ₹10k order for the first 10 days (+-100), ₹30k order for the next 20 days and ₹1 lac order after that (+ – 1000 max for three months, ₹3 lac order (3000) and ₹7 lac order after 7 months lifelong.

STOCK FUTURES, OPTIONS DAILY STRATEGY

Use these 4 screeners for this strategy:

OI increase price rise reversal screener from moneycontrol.com

Weekly breakout nifty100 stocks from the earnometer website.

Bullish for the next day, and

Intraday buying seen in the last 15 minutes from the chartink website.

Keep watching at 9:30 a.m. and 3:10 p.m. Choose stocks that are recovering after a three-month downfall. Say, you buy DLF at ₹347. Check the stock options chain. There should be no gap in the bid-ask price. There is no regular option volume in many stocks. If the volume is okay, then buy DLF futures at ₹347 + buy DLF 340 puts (near out of money + sell 360 call (Option writing). This is the collar strategy, but ₹3 lacs is needed. If you have less capital, then option writing may be avoided.

If you have 70k capital only, then you can opt for the option only combo. But it might easily give you a 1% profit on capital. Buy DLF 350 calls with a premium 15. Then puts should be made with half the premium. Why is this so? If it opens gap up, you will get ₹5 profit in calls against ₹3 loss in puts. Keep studying the FnO historical price on nseindia.com. You should refer to the 10 strategy future course for bigger and safer profits. But focus only on these single strategies and keep records.

Less capital, big profits strategy

See **short term breakout and pocket pivot screener** link from chartink. The capital suggested is 30% of your capital. ₹30,000 from ₹1 lac capital.

Three parameters: Price should be four or three digits. The volume should be in lacs instead of thousands. Review all the data charts within a four-hour time frame. Then one year. Avoid zigzag charts. LTP near day's high even when nifty goes down. If it is in the upper circuit, sell tomorrow. What's a good time to trade? Small volumes in the mornings, bigger volumes in the afternoon. If some stocks are near the circuit limit, then keep stoploss buy at the upper circuit filter price. What if trade turns into a big loss. Let it be. Check blind, tdpower, ndl examples. When there is volume again a week later after recent profit booking, then buy again intraday three times the volume for trade repair. Book in parts and trail stoploss. If stoploss hits due to frequent volatility, then buy small volumes with 50% SL only.

BANK NIFTY STRATEGY

Why bank Nifty? Single focus is more promising. ₹5000 capital may be enough. Optimum capital is ₹30,000. This is the most dynamic strategy, because your capital is always free and the risk is minimal.

Bank Nifty WEEKLY strategy

Go to earnometer. Check up breakouts and down breakouts. Set buy order in most active OTM call and put at previous day's high. See the most active bank Nifty call-put in the money control app. Or Google search to find many such websites.

The maximum capital needed is ₹20,000 for 1-1 lot orders. Expected 22 days. Two big profits worth 500 points. (250 points each)

10 average profits worth 700 points (50 to 80 points each)

10 days no profit loss (5 SL = 5 small targets).

Total 1200 points * 25 = 30,000 per month

Orders should be placed daily with 40 points target if you cannot be at the screen. If you can, then keep flexible targets. Set buy in bank nifty futures if you have enough capital.

What to do, if it is gap up or gap down opening?

If gap up is beyond up breakout, then bank Nifty is bullish after a dip. Keep buy in most active OTM call at previous day's high. If it is gap down, then it will continue to fall after a short covering. Keep buy in most active OTM put at the previous day's high. At the same time, keep an eye on the monthly highs and lows for broad range breakouts. Once a month will be enough for 15 to 20% ROI. This means 200% annually.

Only monthly breakouts can give you ₹2 lacs on ₹1 lac capital. But you can focus when you are not doing anything else.

Three SL action plans for weekly / monthly breakout only, not for the previous day's breakout. Book small profits and set SL buy at newly made day's high. SL 40 points * 25 = 1000. One, on break out. Two, till 11:30 a.m. Three, 1:25 p.m.

Less trades means more net profits. Option writing needs big capital, but many traders don't have that. You need buying only and unidirectional clarity. The underlying five-day chart is a must. Study the EOD analysis, S2/R2, down breakout and up breakout from chartink and the technical summary at investing.com. Historical price study (NSE India) is very good for post-market study. You need a particular time which has a greater probability of movement.

One trade daily is okay. Maximum, two trades a day.

NIFTY – BANKNIFTY MIDDAY BREAKOUT STRATEGY

Intraday traders suffer the biggest losses when nifty / bank nifty shows sudden reversal in the second half of the day. The market remains in a tight range between 11.30 a.m. and 1:30 p.m. generally, waiting for clues from the European market and further direction when it opens. From 11:15 to 1:15 p.m. is the Nifty and bank Nifty range. Resistance and support are tested till this time. So it helps. See the Nifty chart for these ranges. Say nifty has a high of ₹16,680 and the lowest price is at ₹16,610 between this time slot (11.15 a.m. to 1:15 p.m.). Keep the nearest OTM call at ₹16,700 and put at ₹16,600 on the market watch ready. If the **NIFTY** range is broken upside, buy nifty call OTM or as per capital SL 8 points, 8 points * 50 = ₹400.

If **Bank nifty** shows down breakout, buy bank Nifty put OTM or capital wise SL 30 * 25 = ₹750 only.

Bank Nifty REVERSAL strategy

Keep watching reversals. After a three-day downfall, Nifty or bank Nifty is

1. Above ATP

2. Near the day's high

3. Buyers are increasing

If you see that **open-low** is the same in some call/put strike prices, after a big downfall, then **only buy** in the morning. Use Nifty 8 points SL and bank nifty 30 points stoploss, then buy the most active call with a premium of 150 and put worth a 70 point premium for BTST.

Buy at 3:20 p.m. Intraday disturbances are not there. Hedging is suggested overnight. The buying direction is clear, hence biased. Even in a falling market, the Index opens gap up most of the time and falls further from there. There should be a clear outline for targets. If capital engaged is ₹20,000, then 600 is 3% ROI daily. It will give ₹3000 someday by default if you follow the system regular without major disturbances due to greed or FEAR. Practice with single lots for 30 days, three lots for the next 60 days and five lots for the next 90 days, 10 lots for the next 120 days. Ten lots means 5000 daily. You will only need 1% daily. It will give 200% ROI. It can give you returns of ₹100 crores with an investment of just of ₹10k in just 10 years if you invest daily in reliable stocks like ICICI bank and LT through equity SIP. Such stocks can be picked from the top 10 MF holdings.

If you see that Nifty or bank Nifty breaks weekly or reaches a monthly high, then set buy at the day's high of OTM call once again after regular profit booking. Break monthly/weekly lows in a similar way. Buy puts at the day's high but with strict SL. Why? Because it stops overtrading. It also stops disturbances in your day-to-day regular life.

Three mistakes to avoid with the above strategy:

You get carried away by the momentum.

SL/target hits very quickly and you react to cover losses or multiply profits.

The market is volatile and rangebound for 70% of the days.

Nifty monthly profit calculation

There are 22 trading days in a month.

Midday breakout three days 0.3 to 1% profit 50 to 150 points

9 days 0.1 to 0.2% profits 15 to 30 points

10 days exit (loss of brokerage + taxes)

NIFTY is 17,000. So 1% is 170 points. 0.1% is 17 points.

Total expected:

150 to 400 points in 3 days

150 to 300 points in 9 days

-50 points in 10 days

TOTAL= 450 points in 22 days

which works out to 20 points per day

20*lot size 50 = 1000 per day.

There are three weekly breakouts from 22 trading days in a month.

Three days 0.5 to 2% profits 100 to 300 points.

These three big moves may be average or very huge sometimes, as given below.

Total expected:

100 points + 150 points + 150 points = 400 points

Three breakouts in a month would yield

400 * lot size 50 = 20,000 in a month.

Capital requirements

30 to 70k for two MIS orders in Nifty Futures

Expected 20k + 20k = 40k

Two conditions are mandatory to assure this profit: Order placing should be regular. The trader should not miss this even for a single morning or afternoon. Try to exit cost to cost 10 out of 22 days on false breakout. It will turn into mini losses, whatever you try. No one can earn ₹1000 profit regularly.

So finally, you can earn ₹40k per month, which works out to 40k*12 = ₹4.8 lac annually. 1000% profit on ₹48,000 capital. You can search for a broker who will allow you to trade in Nifty MIS intraday with 20k margin per lot only.

OPTION (CALL+PUT) BALANCING for continuous rally or downfall

Suppose you bought bank Nifty option long strangle before some big event or after a long tight range. You bought 31500 calls at ₹300 premium. You bought 31000 puts at ₹300 premium. The total investment 600 points * lot size 25 = ₹15,000.

You are ready here for any big movement on either side. Now bank Nifty moves from 31,200 to 31,500 due to some positive trigger. So, call premium has increased from 300 to 520. Put premium has reduced from 300 to 120 only. Total is 520 + 120 = 640 now.

I expect bank Nifty to go to 32000, and then to 33000 from today's level of 31500 in the coming week. But there will be profit booking after every upside move. So if there is a technical correction of 150 to 300 points only (0.5 to 1%) what will happen? Call will reduce to 50 to 60% (520 to 230). Put will increase by 50 to 70% . Because now put has become far out of money. Put gained 60% from 120 to 200 but call has reduced by 70% from 520 to 230. So total is 200 + 230 = 430 now, 210 points less than the previous day's total.

You need to re balance your position. So, sell the long strangle, both calls and puts at 640. And buy a new combination based on the latest perspective. If there was a bull run in bank Nifty for the last three days, selling is expected more than further buying. So you can buy a bigger put with a smaller OTM call now. At 31,500, you bought 31,400 put at ₹250 premium and bought 31,800 call at ₹200 premium.

If there is a 200 point downfall, the Put may rise from 250 to 380 and the Call may reduce from 200 to 120. Now, the total is 500. You can sell the combo and rebalance again. Calls and puts are chosen on the basis of premium, not on the basis of the strike price.

If you follow a five-day high/low and the Mid-day breakout strategy daily, along with such long strangle, you will be safe in any sudden reversal.

5% daily midcap small cap strategy for fastest profits

Midcap and small caps run after a two-day large cap rally. When there is a normal rally, take smaller volume. When midcap and small cap runs on negative for the day, then you can buy big volumes. Check these two screeners given in the description of the strategy video. Short term breakout and stocks with rising volumes.

Practical demo on how to pick stocks. This screener brings all the winning difference.

If there are volumes in thousands only, you can avoid it. But if the stock price is more than in thousands, then a small quantity should be bought even after a small volume of thousands. Midcap and small cap shares open gap up generally. They show a deceiving rally in the morning and fall sharply from highs in the afternoon. So buy a very small quantity in the morning with 1% SL and 70% quantity. I suggest you buy the stock that emerges after 1:30 p.m. with sector support. Keep 1% SL in half quantity 50%.

If there is no big downfall in nifty or Sensex, then you will earn huge profits. If there is a sudden big downfall, then you are out of 50% quantity. Now, you will be able to buy the same stock or any other emerging stock from the same screener to recover losses.

I suggest you look at top midcap and small cap mutual funds top holdings and Trendlyne MF FII holdings in midcap and small cap stocks for parallel study to pick two great stocks in five seconds from the list of 30 to 50 stocks.

Don't worry about making mistakes or taking the wrong decision. Don't keep staring at the screen for one or two hours. Pick one stock, buy it, set SL for 50% quantity and leave it. It will be sold automatically by RMS if you don't get time to sell before 3:00 p.m. Many of these stocks are not allowed to trade intraday, you need to buy in cash or delivery. Then sell 70% today, sell the remaining the following day. If the stock is near the upper circuit, sell 20% only and get ready the next day on the dot at 9:15 a.m. Stocks with upper circuit filter (only buyer) opens with huge gap up followed by quick profit booking.

Mistakes

- Keep averaging the same falling stock.

- Keep short selling the gaining stocks early and facing big losses from the last big green candle.

- Not giving yourself a chance to make profits big enough to cover three losses in one good trade.

- You don't set stoploss even with 50% quantity.

- You wait for the recovery of a particular stock, missing all the other golden opportunities.

- Impulsive volumes without any logic. If you got 12000 in 1000 shares, then you buy 2000 shares the next day. It should be 200 shares only after a big rally with proper logic.

- You don't exit when Nifty, Sensex breaks weekly low.

If you see one stock gaining by 12% and another losing by 5% then the net return is +12-5 = 7%. Exit all and wait for Nifty, Sensex correction for a safe big trade. Or Book 70% of gaining and 50% of losing stocks to get further profits. The first option is better with my experience. Exit all once is less confusing.

How to accomplish swing trading with stock futures and options hedging?

In the case of stock futures, traders are unable to buy in parts, so they need to buy with reversal strategy or weekly breakout. The capital required is ₹2 lacs for stock futures + ₹1 lac for collar position and ₹2 lacs extra for trade repairs and churning with equity cash. I bought Bharti airtel 1 future (lot size 1851) at 434 future price + sold 450 call + bought 430 put with stoploss at the day's low.

OPTION TRADE REPAIR

BUY oversold stock option first of all only on reversal .

Buy Index option on five day breakout. Sell loss-making calls if sector is negative. Sell loss-making puts if sector is positive. And keep buy at day's high or ATP. Now observe the direction of Nifty. There will be some clear gainers with sector support. Or clear losers in losing sectors. You buy SBI 230 call and it falls to 205. Now keep buy at 210. You can change the instrument between futures or equity cash. In the last two days, you can buy next month at high and current month at bargain price with SL. Use equity or futures near expiry, replacing options. Never cover losses in a single shot. If NIFTY/Bank nifty are in tight range, then switch to stocks. If some stock is volatile then go for Index if there is a clear break out. See the direction on five days breakout or Reversal after three days of continuous fall or rise. No stock moves just after a fall or rise. There will be range or volatility, so premium decay will be there. Thus, make a bull call spread or bear put spread. But at the same time, keep stoploss buy at the day's high in ATM call/put. It will become 1 call BUY+1call sold + 1 put BUY after negative breakout to cover the opposite direction. Make a long strangle on breakout. Notice all these positions. Book when M2M (mark to market) gives a 50% recovery of losses on big moves either side.

CURRENCY TRADING CAPSULE COURSE

USD, INR weekly strategy

You should avoid frequent trading to avoid the fear, greed trap. Focus on the weekly breakout.

You can use the following websites for Currency charts and analysis of four main currency pairs listed in the NSE currency market:

USD-INR, EUR-INR, GBP-INR, JPY-INR

Earnometer.com

In.investing.com

Moneycontrol app

Barchart.com

See weekly high-low in USD – INR. See UP breakout. Place stoploss buy at high. See down breakout. Place stoploss sell at down break out.

When to place an order? Within 30 minutes of the market opening till close. One trade will activate in eight to 10 days. Three trades, in a month. This can give you 20 to 30% of your capital easily (30 * 12 = 300 to 400 percent a year).

Traders needs 2 to 4% margin only for MIS orders in currency, so it is possible to place eight orders in all four currency pairs.

Four BUY orders on weekly high and four SELL orders on weekly low breakout in small capital.

One can get 4 to 7% weekly ROI if 1 to 2 trades activate due to high leverage.

OPTIONS WRITING STRATEGY

Index (nifty – bank nifty options writing)

Options writing gives you profit 70% of the time while options buying gives you profit 30% of the time only. Write weekly on Thursday morning, if the last five days don't show a tight range. Otherwise go for a short butterfly and buy at high in running session.

SELL near OTM call + put and BUY far OTM call + put.

Stock options writing

If the last three days show big moves on either side, check the weekly gainers/losers. Go to the option chain and IV. Sell far out of money call / put of less IV strike price. Keep SL at the day's high to stop unlimited losses. Keep SL at low of the last three days gainers and losers. It will give you big margins. If you don't have, then track manually or place orders in 1-1 share. Write call or sell call on negative breakout, write PUT on positive breakout. Stock option writing is good during the third and fourth week, near expiry, due to fast premium decay. Option buying should be avoided here without any strong clear breakout.

If Nifty futures has been moving upward over the last three days continuously, then place stoploss sell at day's low everyday till it reverses. If it falls continuously, then Place SL buy at the day's high everyday till it shows a sudden, big, sharp reversal.

BTST (Buy Today Sell Tomorrow)

If Nifty futures closes near the day's high with increasing volume after 3:25 p.m. buy it at 3:28 p.m. Buy an OTM put for overnight hedging.

STBT (Sell Today Buy Tomorrow)

Sell Nifty futures at 3:28 p.m. if it closes just near the day's low with increasing volume. And buy OTM call for overnight hedging.

For NIFTY options, choose the nearest out of money OTM call and put strike price and list it in your trading software MarketWatch. If you have more than ₹1 lac capital, focus on call/put writing – short selling at low. If you have ₹20,000 only, then buy call on positive breakout and buy put at negative breakout.

Nifty call, put balancing for bigger rallies

Suppose you bought Nifty option long strangle before some big event or after a long tight range. You bought 17800 calls at ₹300 premium and 17600 puts at ₹300 premium. Total investment: 600 points*lot size 50 = ₹30,000.

You are ready here for any big movement on either side. Now, Nifty moves from 17800 to 18300 due to some positive trigger. So, call premium has increased from 300 to 520. Put premium has reduced from 300 to 120 only. Total is 520 + 120 = 640 now. You expect Nifty to go up to 19,000 from the current level of 18,000, in the coming wcck. But there will be profit booking after every upside move. So if there is a technical correction of 150 to 300 points only (0.5 to 1%) what will happen? Call will reduce by 50 to 60% (520 to 230). Put will increase by 50 to 70% (130 to 200) because now put has become far out of money. So the total is 200 + 230 = 430 now (210 points less than the previous day's total). You need to re balance your position. So, sell the long strangle, both calls put at 640. And buy a new combination with the latest perspective. If there's a bull run in Nifty for the last three days, selling is expected more than further buying. So, you can buy a bigger put with smaller OTM call now. So, at 18300, you bought 18200 put at ₹250 premium and bought 18700 calls at ₹200 premium. If there is a 200 point downfall, the put may rise from 250 to 380. Call may reduce from 200 to 120.

Now, the total is 500. You can sell the combo and rebalance again. Calls and puts are chosen on the basis of premium, not on the basis of strike price. If you follow the five-days high/low and Mid-day breakout strategy daily, parallel to such long strangle, you will be safe in any sudden reversal.

Nifty / Bank Nifty daily TWICE strategy

You need a strategy which is so simple to recall in tough times. There are sudden unexpected fluctuations most of the times.

Buy Nifty June Future + sell nifty July FUT at 9:53 a.m. SL 10 points.

If there is a nine to 10 point move only and SL hits on the other side, exit right then. Options for traders with less capital: Buy nifty OTM call 17800 + buy Nifty OTM put 17600 at 9:53 a.m. SL 8 points on both sides.

Repeat the above at 1:53 p.m. Focus on the early EXIT always. The rest will be done automatically. Buy bank nifty this month, sell bank nifty next month at 9:53 a.m. SL 30 points on both sides. Repeat the same at 2:28 p.m.

Don't trade bank nifty regularly like NIFTY. Trade bank nifty options and futures always after two days of continuous rise or fall.

Bank Nifty options: Buy bank nifty most active OTM call + buy most active OTM put at 9:53 a.m. SL 30 points. Repeat the same at 2:28 p.m. Do not wait till stoploss hits on both sides.

REVERSAL STRATEGY

Just track the last three days continuous losers or gainer from the weekly losers / gainers. Reversals give the best range for the biggest and fastest intraday profits. Set stoploss buy at the day's high in two loser stocks. Keep stoploss sell at the day's low in two gainer stocks. If the trade activates, then place stop loss of 0.5% of the price. Even if the trade activates twice a week, it will give 5 to 6% profits which is more than regular intraday. If you trade in stock options, then place defensive buying. Say, if it is 11, then keep bargain buy at 10 with SL 0.5 points only. If you trade in stock futures then short sell defensive. Say zeel is 170, then place defensive sell at 171.5 with SL at 172.

You can use two screeners to track reversals.

Recovery from intraday low.

Fall from intraday high from NDTV profit.

BANK NIFTY DAILY & POSITIONAL STRATEGY

There are two ways to trade in bank nifty.

For daily trading

Buy bank nifty this month + sell next month at 9:53 a.m. and at 1:53 p.m. with SL 30 points on both sides. If there is a big move than you will gain profits on either side.

For positional trade

Check weekly highs and lows at Earnometer.com or the Moneycontrol app. Keep buy at weekly high and sell at weekly low, so that the trade will be activated once a week. If you trade daily, then there will be a huge tax and brokerage fee due to uncontrolled overreacting. If you get 0.5% (150 points) once a week, this works out to 500 points a month. ₹12,000 to ₹15,000 on ₹1 lac capital is easily possible with weekly trade. Extra 500 points will be maintained with daily trade twice only. If SL hits once in the morning, don't repeat the trade impulsively on the same day.

Why this strategy?

Momentum is the biggest problem. You are trapped in greed and fear and end up with losses. It disturbs your personal, professional life, health and peace of mind. Brokerage fees and taxes are a hidden threat.

DAILY CHURNING STRATEGY IN 1 EVERGREEN STRONG STOCK

Churning means taking butter out of milk but the milk still remains there.

In the same way, the trader cum investor holds two very strong stocks.

If those two stocks might open gap up or gap down, the trader sells 30 to 60% of his holding in MIS intraday with 1% stoploss and tries to book 1 to 2% profit daily. Choose two stocks only. BUY and hold these two stocks with 60% of your capital. Two oversold stocks from two different sectors.

Selection tools-

Darvas scan

Topstock research Bollinger support Or

Oversold stock from trendline

NIFTY100 monthly losers.

Why is this strategy useful?

Gap up opening.

No overtrading.

Focus on deep technicals.

Contrarian sectors perform even if Nifty shows regular long correction.

Cons

Gap down.

Shows loss till reversals.

Lots of confusion in a volatile market.

Goal:

0.5% on capital invested with daily churning (not regular but average)

That allows for 0.5% * 250 trading days = 125%.

If the stock closes near a five-day low or nifty breaks the five-day low and closes near the day's low without recovery, then sell at least 30 to 50% of your holding.

What happens if you are wrong? There is nothing wrong if you have cash in hand. You can engage with a better performing stock for a while. You can switch to some other sector after every quarter. Take 30% of your total capital if NIFTY is near the three-month high. Add 30 to 40% if there is a dip within four to six months.

Don't ever sell all of your holdings in one shot. If there is clear negativity, I suggest you sell 70 to 80% but at least SL buy high in half of the sold quantity. After a two-day continuous upside or downside move, there will be double edged volatility so go with 20 to 30% of your holdings only.

HOW to balance STOCK, FnO, commodity and currency trades by a single trader profitably?

Stock: One trade a day Darwas scan. Stocks with big range highest price. See weekly high/low (earnometer) or the three-day continuous rally or correction. Book profits on the same day.

NIFTY future (Single trade a day) or

Nifty option buying (Open-low same)

Option writing if you have enough capital with open high same.

Banknifty future (One trade a week)

Banknifty option buying with open low same screener.

Option writing open high same from the nsewin.in website.

Commodity: daily 6:00 to 7:00 p.m. or ONCE a week is BEST.

Eight mcx scrips (bullion/base/energy) daily bi directional hedging.

Currency (once a week by placing stoploss LIMIT orders daily. Earnometer 4 pairs **USD/GBP/EUR/JPY – INR.**

Just get a three-in-one account. Place stock/currency in the morning and Commodity in the evening if capital is less.

Ek TOWN me hokar bhi Mumbaikar or Newyorker se aage kaise honge?

(Sidhi DIL ki baat HINGLISH me)

India ki badi abadi gaon me rehti he. Kai log kheti karte he, kuchh log dukan chalate hai. Kisi ko baahar aane ka permission nhi mila, To kuchh ghar sambhalane ke liye wahi ruk gye. Ek zamana tha jab chhoti jagah ka aadami badi city ke logon ke pichhe hi chalta tha. Kyuki aage badhne ke saare avsar, mauke, jobs aur jankari shahar me hi thi. Lekin ab shahron me dhakke jyada aur mauke kam milte he. Fir bhi success stories to abhi bhi cities me hi mil rahi he. Kyon? Abhi bharosa jaga nhi he puri tarah.

Soch ya trend dhire se badlate he.

Apko apne gaon me hi ye 6 change apnane honge.

1. **time pass ke liye internet ka use mat karo.** Sikhne ke liye youtube, whatsapp, facebook, instagram ka use karo. Jab thak jao to achchha content, webseries, cokestudio, Pinkfloyd se chhota sa break le lo. Lekin fir se lag jao kaam par.

2. **city me rehne par maintanance** 15000 jata he to 4000 gaon me hi sikhne par kharch karo. Koi online paid course, Digital marketing, editing, achchi data speed, netflix, amazon prime ka subscription.

3. **English ka howwa bhul jao**. Ek sahi group ka sahara lo, aage chalo.

   Waise to hindi me kafi kuchh he hi.Youtube par kai free courses he.

4. **mahine me 2 travel** karna hi he. Pure india me aur ho sake to globe me connection banao. Upyogi banna padega. Apke paas kuchh to aisa hoga jo ya to unhe mazedar lage ya unke kaam ka ho. Apko shoping mall lubhate he to unhe khet lubhate he. apko scotch lubhati he to unko taadi/feni ka chaska hoga.

5. **Toxic / Time killers se bacho,**

   Jinke jaisa nhi banna, unke saath kam waqt guzaro. Jinke jaisa banane ka sapna he, unke liye waqt nikalo. Kai log tumhe validation nahi denge par faansi par to nhi latkayenge.

6. **jinko benchmark manoge, unke pichhe chaloge**, toh saare globe ko hi dekho suno, google earth, travelxp, fashion, business sab aapke hath me he. Apka dimag bhi original ya naya soch sakta he, bas apne aap me inferiority mat aane do. Kyunki fir iski reaction me hum superiority dikhane lagte he. Kya he, city walon me aisa khaas. Aapke pass kya zyada he? Jyada spare time, kyunki aap line me nhi lage ho. kam survival expense, Identity he aapke pass. Unko identity apke paas ake milti he. Unhe bas ye jyada pata he ki kaun si local kaha jati he? Saaf paani hawa, khule ghar toh hai, bas dimag ki khidki kholna he.

Trading Tricks

1. Try to buy in red blink and sell in blue blink always.

2. Keep checking net position of all clients by pressing ALT+f6 every 10 minutes. Book profits from there directly.

3. Trade huge volumes with limit price only and keep booking part profit. Sell big parts first to take control. Don't trade big volumes with market price order.

4. Keep buying orders in dips with very small stop losses in series order strategy. Keep selling them in series as well.

5. Keep strict stop loss on all trades. Ask the client to set SL and tell them every trade must have stop loss for half the quantity at least.

6. Keep stop loss buying above high in top gainers and stop loss selling in top losers with profit booking order with 0.5% (trading robot model).

7. If any stock dips suddenly, then change the order later, buy/sell it first.

8. If there is very small gap in order price and current price, then sell by changing order only.

9. Use f3-F3 to keep checking the order book and keep deleting all useless orders from time to time. Use shift+F3 to cancel ALL orders daily at 3:29 p.m. before the market closes or during any crisis.

10. Keep experimenting with new strategies with low volume and show it to your clients. Your turnover will grow with safety.

11. Hedging protects your clients and doubles your turnover and that of the brokerage firm.

12. Sometimes, dealers may stop their clients from booking profits. It is more important to protect them from losses instead of earning more profits.

13. It is good to speak less. Your every word can affect a trader's sentiments, so don't speak more than is essential.

14. Keep buying orders in dips with SL for falling stocks and sell them fast on jumps.

15. Buy strong closing stocks for BTST at 3:29 p.m. and sell it the next day at 9:16 a.m. Keep prior off market order before 9:00 p.m. if it is possible.

16. Promote two small trades for each with strict stoploss. Buy top gainers and sell top losers.

17. If the internet speed is slow then buy or sell 1-1 stock and check current price first before a big trade. It happens generally in the odin diet.

18. Continue to buy with stop loss in top six gainers just before the circuit filter from volume increase price rise screener. If two of them are activated and remain on the upper circuit till close, it will open gap up (3 to 6%) the next day.

BACK-OFFICE REPORTS

An online trader need not maintain his accounts on his own. Everyone is scared of lengthy accounts in any business. All these accounts are maintained by the main broker's software which takes 10 minutes of the sub broker/trader's time to check everything. This is the only business where your accounting and documentation are done by staff whom you don't pay at all. I have given the details of a general back-office software which may have some variation from one broking firm to another. One can see reports by entering the user ID and password on the broker's official website.

Share Accounting-

Management reports

    RMS – client funding

    Fund summary

    RMS reports

    RMS stock reports

    Click fund summary first.

    Choose sub broker or client option.

    Enter name and fetch details.

    RMS report will help you manage bad debt clients who have greater debits than their stock value.

    RMS stock reports will show client-wise or scrip-wise holdings.

    Scrip-wise holding will help you to act accordingly during a crisis in any particular company stock.

MASTERS

Go to the client details and see all the personal details like name, address, mail ID or phone number to inform them properly. Lack of communication and misinformation is the basic problem when it comes to small level broking in India.

SHARE TRANSACTION

Contract Printing

STT report

Contract notes are printed by the HO of every client and sent to the sub broker or to the client's mail ID in digital format. STT report (10DB) is needed when clients file income tax returns.

SHARE REPORTS

Delivery reports

New reports

Settlement summary

Turnover Brokerage

Enter settlement number 2015003 to 2015190. The Settlement number is made up of the year and trading day counting. The example above shows the third day to the 190th trading day of the year 2015. Enter scrip name: DLF. Enter party code or date option and submit details. You can find buy/sell rate of any share, open position (hold quantity) and the average rate of that scrip.

Turnover brokerage

Enter date. Enter sub broker's name. Choose date and summary and

submit. It will show intraday and delivery brokerage details day-to-day.

FINANCE REPORTS

Daily report view: Enter party code (from and to) and date in all the segment party ledgers. You can watch and analyse the total business after seeing all these reports regularly. You can know the amount you earn every day. A few businesses can show this with such clarity. These 10 minutes of back office work is very important. You can delegate all your work to a terminal operator (dealer) or marketing executive but you can't avoid these 10 minutes for proper risk management. Lack of management will not reduce your income but it may create huge losses which can't be recovered in the next five to 10 years. That's why the broking business is very simple after detailed training but very risky without total knowledge of the market and the business. Even a good trader may not be as successful as a good sub-broker. A successful sub broker should be a good trader but it's not essential. That is a completely different line of work.

10 steps to become a successful day trader

Stock market, commodity, crypto currency

> Self-assessment (SWOT analysis)
>
> Arrange capital
>
> Open a trading account
>
> Practice using the software on your smartphone
>
> Choose the right strategy
>
> Start your study with TV channels, websites
>
> Back test with small volume
>
> Set time-wise goals

You need not quit your job right now.

Don't assume that you need to be on the trading screen from morning to evening. A trader who watches the trading screen for an hour a day can be successful.

Do's of Intraday trading

Fix a right time suitable for you. Trade the right volume with strict SL and leave. Don't react or change plans after losses or profits.

Don'ts of INTRADAY trading

Favourite stocks reaction on every up and down. Welcome all the noise and overstudy the market.

Three option mistakes

Limited to less capital and index options only, but big profits expected.

Trading stock options without hedging and clear breakout from screeners.

Not booking reasonable profits that have already been calculated.

Four mistakes of bank nifty futures

- Overtrading due to frequent temptation

- No hedging with options

- Big moves every four months confuse the trader for the next three months.

- Optimum profit calculations should be there.

Don'ts of swing trading

- Picking the wrong stocks without screeners or impulsive buying in rally.

- Buying in one shot instead of 1/2/3 ratio.

- Not giving reasonable time.

- No optimum returns calculated; say 3% in three days through the all-in-one screener strategy.

Don'ts of cryptocurrency trade

- Trading big capital in one shot.

- Running after any new coin hearing the success story of some other coin. No proper target calculated.

- Registering with an unreliable broker.